a **LIVING**|**FREE** guide

Home Butchering Handbook

Jamie Waldron and Angela England

ALPHA
A member of Penguin Group (USA) Inc.

ALPHA BOOKS

Published by the Penguin Group (USA) Inc.

Penguin Group (USA) Inc., 375 Hudson Street, New York, New York 10014, USA • Penguin Group (Canada), 90 Eglinton Avenue East, Suite 700, Toronto, Ontario M4P 2Y3, Canada (a division of Pearson Penguin Canada Inc.) • Penguin Books Ltd., 80 Strand, London WC2R 0RL, England • Penguin Ireland, 25 St. Stephen's Green, Dublin 2, Ireland (a division of Penguin Books Ltd.) • Penguin Group (Australia), 250 Camberwell Road, Camberwell, Victoria 3124, Australia (a division of Pearson Australia Group Pty. Ltd.) • Penguin Books India Pvt. Ltd., 11 Community Centre, Panchsheel Park, New Delhi—110 017, India • Penguin Group (NZ), 67 Apollo Drive, Rosedale, North Shore, Auckland 1311, New Zealand (a division of Pearson New Zealand Ltd.) • Penguin Books (South Africa) (Pty.) Ltd., 24 Sturdee Avenue, Rosebank, Johannesburg 2196, South Africa • Penguin Books Ltd., Registered Offices: 80 Strand, London WC2R 0RL, England

International Standard Book Number: 978-1-61564-2-137
Library of Congress Catalog Card Number: 2013933133

15 14 13   8 7 6 5 4 3 2 1

Interpretation of the printing code: The rightmost number of the first series of numbers is the year of the book's printing; the rightmost number of the second series of numbers is the number of the book's printing. For example, a printing code of 13-1 shows that the first printing occurred in 2013.

Printed in the United States of America

Note: This publication contains the opinions and ideas of its author. It is intended to provide helpful and informative material on the subject matter covered. It is sold with the understanding that the author and publisher are not engaged in rendering professional services in the book. If the reader requires personal assistance or advice, a competent professional should be consulted.

The author and publisher specifically disclaim any responsibility for any liability, loss, or risk, personal or otherwise, which is incurred as a consequence, directly or indirectly, of the use and application of any of the contents of this book.

Trademarks: All terms mentioned in this book that are known to be or are suspected of being trademarks or service marks have been appropriately capitalized. Alpha Books and Penguin Group (USA) Inc. cannot attest to the accuracy of this information. Use of a term in this book should not be regarded as affecting the validity of any trademark or service mark.

Most Alpha books are available at special quantity discounts for bulk purchases for sales promotions, premiums, fundraising, or educational use. Special books, or book excerpts, can also be created to fit specific needs. For details, write: Special Markets, Alpha Books, 375 Hudson Street, New York, NY 10014.

Publisher: *Mike Sanders*

Executive Managing Editor: *Billy Fields*

Senior Acquisitions Editor: *Brook Farling*

Senior Development Editor: *Christy Wagner*

Development Editor: *Nancy D. Lewis*

Senior Production Editor: *Janette Lynn*

Copy Editor: *Cate Schwenk*

Book Designer: *Rebecca Batchelor*

Indexer: *Heather McNeill*

Layout: *Ayanna Lacey*

Proofreader: *Gene Redding*

Photographer: *Mark Horsley*

Illustrations: *Erin Gardner*

Contents

Appendixes

Foreword

There is a yearning amongst some people in modern society for more control over the food they eat. We are inundated with news about food recalls, food poisoning, and the latest chemicals added to food. When we see disturbing, undercover films from packing plants, this only increases the desire for food that is responsibly grown, processed, and brought into our homes. Ultimately, the more consumers do themselves, the more control they have over what they feed themselves and their families.

Modern livestock production is a lightning rod for controversy. Never before in history has society been presented with so much readily available meat, at any time of the year, right at your local supermarket. Today's livestock industry has animals gaining faster and producing more meat and milk than their ancestors ever could have, all to feed a society that expects a constant supply of safe, affordable meat. But are these two objectives compatible? The constant drive to lower costs all along the production chain has consequences. Feeding animals an unnatural diet to increase their rate of gain and raising them in confinement are all normal farm practices that have evolved to fill this need for a constant supply of meat at your local supermarket. As technology has progressed, so has the ability of packing plants to slaughter livestock. Many processors can handle thousands of animals in a single day. It is inevitable, in a production chain that strives to lower costs as much as possible, that animals will sometimes be treated as commodities, not necessarily able to express themselves as they would like.

I am proud to be a cattleman; I enjoy raising cattle and producing beef. On my farm, I graze cattle as much as possible, feeding them in confinement when necessary. I finish cattle on either corn or grass, depending on where they are marketed. Over time, my production practices have evolved to follow the seasons. My cows calve in the spring, out on pasture, with green grass beneath them and blue sky above them. These cows and calves graze grass until winter and are then confined to a yard until spring, when the cows go back out to grass. The cattle that will be grass finished go back to pasture and the cattle that will be corn finished are moved into the feedlot. Whether the cattle are out on pasture, or in confinement, it is very important that they are kept clean, well fed, and content. I believe that cattle that are raised in a low stress environment, kept calm, and handled in a respectful, humane way will not only be happier, healthier cattle, they will also produce more tender, tastier beef.

For consumers wanting to take control of their food supply, all of the information available today must be overwhelming. This book will help anyone who wants to find a source of safe, high quality meat and prepare it themselves—from carcass to freezer. Learning how to cut animals into the portions you want will become routine once it is explained by a highly skilled butcher like Jamie Waldron. For those of us who like to have control over what we eat, knowing how to butcher an animal is a valuable skill that this book will help to explain.

Thank you,

Shawn Morris
Cattleman
Comber, Ontario, Canada

Introduction

The timing for this book couldn't be better. People are interested in how their food is being produced again, and for good reason. Food contaminations, *E. coli* outbreaks, and massive food recalls have brought some very major concerns to the forefront of the food conversation.

This book aims to enable the homesteader, food enthusiast, or newcomer to butchery with an in-depth look at the craft. You'll see it has been experiencing a resurgence in recent years, due in part to the back-to-basics food movement that is taking hold nationwide.

Folks want to have total control over their food; some are frightened by what they hear and read, and with the current state of food production methods, chefs are butchering whole animals at restaurants to ensure total control over quality and costs. Others are simply interested in learning a skill that will empower them to butcher their own livestock and maintain control over which cuts and sizes of cuts they'll have in their freezers. Butchery is a skill that will get better and better with every animal you work on.

Whatever your reason, this book is a gift, from us to you, to share an age-old craft that has proven invaluable for mankind. From first civilizations until now, with our mechanized kill plants that can process some 4,500 head of cattle per day, some balance and respect was lost along the way.

There was a time when slaughtering animals was a yearly happening. When families would gather to give thanks to the animals for providing valuable nourishment, and, in return, they would strive not to waste a single part of that animal. Questions didn't exist back then of how the animals were reared, what they were fed, or how they were handled during slaughter; it was known.

Today's home butcher should be asking those questions. They are the building blocks to a knowledgeable butcher, the foundation to his or her understanding of what he or she is dealing with once that carcass has been laid before them.

Finding good meat shouldn't be hard, and thanks to a younger generation of farmers, good meat is being raised across North America and being reared in a respectful way. So now you can reap the result of efforts and enjoy the quality that they're producing.

You as a home butcher will now be empowered to make the most out of whatever animal it is that will feed you and your loved ones. While every meat species is not covered in this book, the ones that are will provide a base knowledge of other animals of similar muscular and skeletal makeup.

Enjoy,

Jamie & Angela

How This Book is Organized

The *Home Butchering Handbook* is broken down into three specific parts. Each one is organized so that you can find the exact information you are looking for, quickly and easily.

Part 1, The Butchering Craft Past and Present, starts off talking about butchering's long and bloody history. It seems like the further removed from the source we got, the bigger and faster the machine moved, and the worse things became. Thankfully, the tide is turning back, as more people are looking for the personalization that comes from home butchering and locally sourced meats.

It can be confusing when you start your home butchering journey. How do you butcher the large animal before you work it into individual and recognizable cuts? In **Part 2, The Breakdowns**, we show you a sampling of how to do a wide variety of cuts on various animals so you can develop your own unique style.

The cuts you see in the grocery store aisles on square Styrofoam packets are only the bare beginning of what is available to the home butcher. In **Part 3, Butchering Beyond the Cuts**, we explore how to move beyond the basics and create some delicious, country-style foods that require a few additional steps.

There are also three separate appendices: a **Glossary** containing definitions of some butchering terms used in the book, **Resources for More Information** on sourcing meat or additional reading material, and information on **Tying a Butcher's Knot**.

Extras

There are some extra elements throughout the book that you will want to pay special attention to.

A CUT ABOVE

These are tips and tricks from an expert butcher to make your home butchering experience easier. These sidebars are like chatting with a fellow butcher over the work table.

WARNING

These are the things that will get you in trouble if you're not careful! Heed these words of wisdom to stay safe during the process.

DEFINITION

Home butchering—like any new hobby—includes some terminology that may be unfamiliar at first. Read these for the low-down on what's what.

BUTCHER'S TIP

Watch these sidebars for extra how-to's that help you move beyond the basics or fill in extra information you'll need along the way.

Acknowledgments

From Jamie:

Erin Gardner for her never-ending supply of love, support, and artistic talent that shines through in the pages of this book.

Angela England for putting to paper what I could only try to articulate.

Stephen Alexander for showing me what retail butchery is and is going to be, and for the generous use of Cumbrae's Dundas for the photography in this book.

Mark Breach for showing me the how and why of butchery.

George Crawford for taking the time to dissect and explore with me.

Kevin Evelegh and Kyle Forth for their expertise in the kitchen.

Brandon Thurley and his team at Cumbrae's Dundas.

Joe Amaral for seeing a kindred spirit and bringing me into the fold.

Ron and JoAnne Waldron for going above and beyond.

Mark Horsley for his stunning photography.

Chef Fraser Macfarlane of Quatrefoil Restaurant for his masterful work on fish.

Brook and Marilyn, this literally wouldn't have happened without either of you.

My closest friends (you know who you are) and family who put up with my rash and sometimes erratic decisions.

And to all the butchers out there, new and old, who respect tradition, innovation, and most importantly, the craft.

From Angela:

As always, to my loving husband Sidney, who supports me on every step of my amazing and crazy journey.

To my kids, who assure me that other people will like my books, because I am the "bestest talker" in the whole wide world.

To the Lord who brings amazing opportunities my way—may I always be faithful to make the most of them.

Thank you to Jamie for leading the way toward change for the better … locally raised, locally processed, and respectful treatment of those around us. I appreciate his patience and willingness to answer all my questions, texts, and IMs.

And to everyone who has decided to take greater responsibility for their own food—I salute you. May your journey always be an exciting and fulfilling one.

From Alpha:

Alpha Books would like to acknowledge the talents and efforts of Mark Horsley for producing the fine photographs that appear in this book, and Erin Gardner, for her wonderful illustrations.

The Butchering Craft Past and Present

1

Part of understanding why current trends in butchery are so important is exploring the history of the industry. In this part, you'll learn why locally produced meat is the best and how to begin your home butchery journey, in addition to tips on how to set up your butchering workspace along with the necessary tools you'll need to have on hand.

Butchering: The Evolution of a Craft

1

Butchering your own meat used to be a home-based craft in which everyone understood the fundamentals. However, the last 50 years has seen greater centralization and industrialization, and butchering now primarily takes place in meatpacking plants—not to be confused with slaughterhouses, which are where the animals actually die. These packing plants and slaughterhouses now service wide geographical areas and process hundreds of animals each day.

A growing number of people are seeking to return to a more balanced and self-sufficient way of life. They know that the best quality meat is the result of personalized attention. The art of home butchering allows more of the animal to be used, provides quality control through skilled and knowledgeable processing, and often reaps a cost savings for the home butcher who is sourcing high-quality meat at cheaper per-pound prices.

As part of the food revolution we've experienced the last few years, there is a growing trend toward home butchering. Many people are seeking to take greater responsibility for the ethics behind their food. And of course, there is an art of creating the perfect cut specifically tailored to your needs as a foodie that will turn your kitchen into a mini gourmet restaurant.

Learning the techniques of home butchering takes practice. This book will get you started along your journey. Each time you work up another side of beef or other animal, you'll learn something new and become more confident in your skills.

The History of Butchering

How did we get from a farmer butchering what he needed to feed his family that week, to large-scale plants processing enough meat in one day to feed an army? As industrialization and technology transformed the assembly line, these advances were also applied to meatpacking plants.

Before the days of easy refrigeration, meat was usually processed when the weather was cold. Fresh meat could be enjoyed during hard freezes, with the rest of the meat stored by being cured, smoked, or salted. This processing would allow meat to keep through warm months when fresh meat would quickly spoil. Very little was wasted when the animal was processed, a phenomenon that is coming full-circle with head-to-tail butchering techniques making a comeback.

With the advent of the railroad, processing became centralized. Livestock could be shipped to more populated areas and processed in larger amounts. Major meatpacking plants sprang up around the railroad hubs such as Omaha, Kansas City, and Chicago. Cuts would be sold as whole carcasses, sides, or large portions to local butchers who would then cut and sell the preferred cuts to individual customers.

Often these large-scale meatpacking plants were dangerous and filthy. Because of the horrific conditions, the general public began to care about the way their meat was being processed. By the 1920s and 1930s, these packing plants became unionized and created a more balanced, stable situation.

For a time these meatpacking plants were safer environments, and workers were paid enough to earn a middle-class wage. That didn't last for more than a few decades. Once our refrigeration and transportation systems developed to the point where it was easier to process the cuts near the slaughterhouses and ship the meat ready-to-eat, the packing plants moved to more rural areas and conditions changed once again.

Now meatpacking plants have technology that allows more animals to be processed faster than ever. Add to that the fact that workers are underpaid, have extremely high turnover rates, and are often poorly qualified or trained for the job of properly handling raw meat. All of these factors combine to create a dangerous work environment.

WARNING

Recent years have seen increased criticism of the meatpacking industry, which currently has 80 percent of its market share controlled by four main companies. With the lack of competition comes lack of variety, bigger corporate control, and a lack of personalization.

Safety Concerns

One of the biggest concerns with the modern meat-processing plants is the lack of oversight. The United States Department of Agriculture (USDA) is charged with the task of inspecting over 6,000 meatpacking plants. However, they use a program called Hazard Analysis and Critical Control Point (HACCP), which relies on inspections instituted by the plants themselves.

When contaminated meat is discovered, according to the book *Fast Food Nation* by Eric Schlosser (Houghton Mifflin, 2001), the USDA can't immediately shut down the plant or issue a recall.

Instead it contacts the plant and asks how the plant would like to handle it. Of course this time delay can result in additional packages of meat being shipped, sold, and even consumed before an official voluntary recall ever comes down. Fecal contamination, injured workers, and unsanitary tools can all happen with surprising frequency.

The speed at which these meatpacking plants move means cheaper food prices, but with speeds of 300 to 400 cows per hour, it's much more difficult to ensure that each animal is handled as safely as possible. Plants can process thousands of pigs in a day, and the line moves constantly as workers sort the various cuts and parts.

In interviews with workers at processing plants, the estimated time from when a pig carcass leaves the dehairing station (removing the hair from the skin of the pig) to when it is processed into *primal cuts* and sent to the freezer is less than 10 minutes. Recent increases in speed at which this process happens has fueled growing concerns for worker safety, meat quality, and food safety.

DEFINITION

The **primal cuts** are the larger pieces of meat that are initially separated from the carcass. These will go on to become final cuts. For example, a full shoulder would be a primal cut, while the individual roasts, steaks, and chops created later are the final cuts.

This speed creates conditions that result in one of the most dangerous work environments in the United States. In 1998 reports showed that nearly 30 percent of workers sustained a work-related injury, sometimes severe and sometimes fatal. Yet some feel that these numbers are lower than actual injury rates because of the high numbers of immigrants in the workforce. Because of this frightening trend, safety for workers in the commercial field is one politically motivated reason that many consumers are turning to local or self-butchering for their families' food.

Lack of Personalization

When the butchering process moved into or next door to the slaughterhouses instead of staying located in your friendly local neighborhood shop, the lack of personalization was a given. Instead of visiting your local butcher for the week and ordering the cuts you wanted, meatpacking plants shipped identical looking cuts by the truckload. For a while, this was seen as a sign of progress and desirable; everything was so neat and uniform looking.

BUTCHER'S TIP

Your local grocery store might have a "meat cutter" on staff, so perhaps you are wondering how that differs from a true "butcher." A meat cutter is trained usually in one area of disassembly or slicing specific muscles from vacuumed sealed bags. A butcher, on the other hand, is a complete package—so to speak—able to break down an entire animal and process meats further into ground, sausage, or cured portions.

Little Styrofoam shrink-wrapped packs arrived at the grocery store with the choices premade for us. Ground beef, ribs, and steaks are uniform and tidy looking. Clean looking. Sterilized and plastic wrapped. Just like every other package in the entire crate. Informed consumers are beginning to desire personalized care with their food choices, however, which is a driving reason for the return to home butchering.

The Revival of Home Butchering

As more meatpacking plants reach agreements with large-scale cattle producers and company-owned feedlots, the cattle price per head paid to small farmers has decreased. In addition, workers' wages have decreased about $1 per hour in the past 10 years. These savings aren't typically passed on to consumers. Buying directly from a local farmer means more of your spending dollar in the rancher's pocket and increased savings for your family as well.

As more people buy locally sourced meat or even raise their own, these stalwart independent souls take up their cleavers to continue their self-sufficient journey. It is the logical next step for those seeking to sever ties to the status quo and recapture another lost art from generations past.

And of course, as with many DIYs, doing your own cuts can save you money in the kitchen. Sometimes premium cuts or unusual pieces can be difficult to find and are expensive when you do find them. But buying a whole animal carcass or side of beef can often be done for a price that comes out to pennies per pound. Once you break it down yourself, using the techniques in this book, you'll find that you've saved yourself and your family quite a lot.

Selectivity and Personalization

Have you ever met those foodies who are super picky about their cuts of meat? Maybe *you* are that foodie! If you've found yourself losing patience with the selection of meat available at your local grocer, then the answer to your problem may be to do it yourself.

Many of the choices for the types of cuts, qualities of meat, and even pricing are made for you before the meat ever hits the shelves. With Styrofoam squares and vacuum packs, there is little room for custom cuts. The machines are set for efficiency and speed. When breaking down your own meat, you get a chance to hand-select all of these elements, including pricing in most cases.

Another reason foodies and home cooks might want personalization of their meat cuts is because of cultural variations. The traditional American method of breaking down a pig yields relatively few cuts. In other cultures, however, unique types of cuts require more selective and specialized work. It's no wonder that many foodies who want to try traditional cultural dishes or specialty gourmet food turn to home butchering for their meat.

Sourcing Quality Meat

There is a variety of reasons people become involved in home butchering: independence, political beliefs, economics, and controlling cuts for gourmet cooking. Whatever your reasons, you need to find a good source of meat to hone your butchering skills.

Finding high-quality meats may take a bit of effort on your part, and it depends a great deal on your location and the culture of the community you live in. If you're in an area that isn't supporting local farmers, you may have difficulty sourcing meat. You may not have a butcher shop that focuses on local or high-quality meats as their main objective. Also, some areas are without a small-scale slaughterhouse to handle the dispatching of individual animals, which can make it hard to coordinate your purchases with the farmers who raise them.

> **BUTCHER'S TIP**
>
> You can tell a lot about the quality of the meat and how well the animal was fed by looking at the intramuscular fat in the eye of the rib. This trick works for beef, lamb, and pork. When you see an even amount of specks of fat, the animal put on weight reasonably and evenly. When you see large, solid-looking pieces of fat, you know the animal's diet caused rapid weight gain and didn't allow for even fat distribution. This is one of the noticeable differences between grass-finished and traditional feedlot-finished steer, for example.

While there may be a few resources for purchasing responsibly raised meats online, we're here to discuss purchasing whole animals for the purpose of home butchering to your specifications. Using an online store may not provide the opportunity to purchase whole or half carcasses. Inevitably, these purchases are best made in person from relatively local sources.

It may be left to you to secure either whole animals or large primal cuts from area farmers or abattoirs (slaughterhouses). Using a farmer will pretty much ensure that you're getting what you're after. If you know of a custom kill abattoir (a facility that kills a smaller number of animals as opposed to larger kill plants that may slaughter in the thousands per day), then it's up to you to ask some important questions:

- Where is this animal from?
- How was it raised?
- What was its feeding program?
- Did it have access to a pasture or was it confined?
- Will they deliver and perhaps even break your carcass into more manageable primal cuts?

Knowing the breed may or may not be important to you right now, but it is a telltale sign the farmer knows which breeds are best for your climate. This will affect the animal's ability to put on weight at a rate that's normal for that breed.

For many home butchers, finding a local processor who can dispatch the animal for you can be the hardest part. Larger slaughterhouses won't usually handle single animals or promise that you get the meat from a specific animal you want.

Meet Local Farmers

Meeting local farmers in your area is going to be your best bet, hands down. If you're lucky enough to have a farmer's market in your town or somewhere near, it will be easier for you to find them. Also check with local feed stores or veterinarians for ranchers in your area who raise the animals you are interested in. Often times a small rancher may not advertise an animal for sale but would be willing to help you out if you called.

Most farmers are happy to have you come to their place of business and check out how they do things. If they're not, move along.

Farmers, for the most part, are a proud bunch. They like having folks around and educating them on the realities of farming. They will show you how a working farm may not be neatly manicured lawns and shiny tractors. A working farm has dirt; dirty pants, dirty animals, and a need for rubber boots most days. And you'll see that there's a difference between dirt and filth.

And they love talking about their animals. As far as I'm concerned, if the farmer is open with you, takes the time to answer your questions, and shows you where the animals are kept and what they eat, then you've found your source for quality animals.

In the next few chapters of this book, we walk you through common cuts for the most common animals encountered in the home butchery. If this is your first time, we recommend following along with the directions as closely as possible. But once you've established the basic techniques, you'll begin to develop your own style and be able to cut your favorite pieces for the special meals that your family enjoys.

Preparing the Optimum Workspace

Home butchering is a skill that is best done when you have the correct tools and workspace available to you. This doesn't mean you have to spend a fortune on supplies, but rather you need to create a safe environment that is easy to work in. A safe, efficient workspace will be easier to use, and the right tools will make the job of making your own cuts at home possible.

Knives out of place are dangerous to everyone involved. I'm already clumsy enough—I don't need to tempt fate when it comes to sharp objects!

And as any cook can testify, having the tools you need right at hand makes it 10 times easier to prepare a meal; likewise for the home butcher. You want to have the right tools in the right place. As my dad used to say, "A place for everything and everything in its place."

Counter Space

Give yourself plenty of space when you are working to prepare home butchering cuts. Make sure your countertop or table is a comfortable height. A good average is about 3 feet tall. You want the counter level just about hip level or a little lower so you'll have good leverage when making your cuts.

Expect to use at least 5 feet of space. You will find yourself working much more effectively if you can spread out. And for larger sides like beef or pork, you'll want the counter or island space to be wide enough to hold the entire side. That means closer to 3 feet deep and 5 feet long at the minimum.

The counter or butchering block needs to be not only spacious, but easy to clean as well. Plastic and wood are the most commonly used cutting surfaces. While wood is the traditional surface, care must be taken with both to sanitize properly while you work.

Workspace Necessities

When you are working with meat, you want to make sure you have a few items close at hand. Soap, bleach, and both hot and cold running water are needed for a kitchen or kitchen-like area to be sanitary.

Keep a couple of garbage cans nearby for the waste pieces and *offal*. Find out what your local waste disposal requirements are, as some cities have strict rules about what to do with meat waste products. Others allow you to simply compost them or take them to the landfill.

DEFINITION

Offal is considered to be the inedible parts of a butchered animal, such as organ meats and overlooked products generally gathered during the evisceration process (liver, heart, kidneys, intestines, etc.).

In addition to the trash can, you'll want clean and sanitized bins to hold the useable pieces you are producing as you work. These should be in a variety of sizes, depending on the size of the animal you're working and what you plan to keep. If you plan to use bones for stock, you'll need larger tubs, but meat trimmings won't take up as much room.

Store like items together; for example, keep usable fat in one container, stock bones in another container, and so on. When butchering meat yourself, the cuts are just the first step before the rest of the processing for the final cuts. Have a place dedicated to those extra bits as you work so you don't have to stop the flow of work as you break the animals down.

Have your knives, saw, cleaver, breaking hook, and other tools clean, organized, and easily accessible. Just being aware of your tools will go a long way toward preventing injury or accidentally cutting yourself.

Fridge and Freezer Space

If you are used to buying a week's worth of groceries at a time, butchering a whole animal is going to be a shock to you and your freezer. Make sure you clear enough space in your fridge and freezer to devote to the meat you are working with. With multiple animals or larger animals like beef, you'll need a lot of room.

When evaluating your freezer needs for your family, consider that in general, 1 cubic foot of freezer space will hold 30 to 32 pounds of meat. So a small 7 cubic foot chest freezer will hold about 200 pounds of meat. This would be about the same as one deer and a few chickens. A 14 cubic foot freezer will hold over 400 pounds of meat. This would be about what you could easily expect to get from a cow.

Remember that you will also need room in your refrigerator or freezer to store the meat you are working with. When you section your carcass into large sections of meat, you'll want to store those sections temporarily. For example, once you section a lamb (see Chapter 4) into the primal cuts, you'll want to store those portions in a cool place while you work up the individual cuts for long-term storage.

Especially with meat like pork and chicken, you'll want to keep the temperatures down into a safe zone that will prevent contamination from harmful bacteria. If you cannot immediately work on the meat, place it in the fridge until you can come back to it. The USDA considers any temperatures between 40–140°F to be the Danger Zone, or temperatures at which bacteria can grow rapidly.

The Essential Tools

As you can imagine, there are a lot of tools that make it easier to work your own cuts of meat. Each item on this list is important and should be considered necessary. Invest in good quality tools because they will hold up better than cheap ones, and you'll actually save money in the long run.

There are lots of tools that could be considered fun tools or luxury items that aren't needed. For example, a band saw could be useful for cutting porterhouse steaks or pork chops more quickly, but you can use a hand saw just fine without the expense associated with the larger tools. If you are looking to add to your repertoire of implements, a few of these items are listed in the section, "The Extra Stuff," at the end of the chapter.

BUTCHER'S TIP

Like Batman with his utility belt, the knife scabbard is the tool belt of butchers. There are several materials you could use, such as plastic or aluminum, and they will keep the knives right at your side for easy reach. The scabbard protects your knives, keeps them safely in one place, and prevents you from accidentally slicing yourself.

Boning Knives

There are a variety of shapes and sizes available, so you might try a few different knives to see which you prefer. Many butchers prefer a semi-stiff, curved blade about 5 inches long because it gives them good control when removing bones.

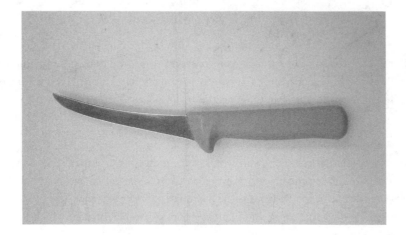

Boning knives are highly flexible tools and are used often throughout the butchering process, so don't skimp on a cheap blade. Expect to spend around $30 or more for a decent blade that sharpens well and fits your hand comfortably. We've seen both plastic and wooden handles, but both should be well made and easy to clean.

Cimeter Knives

A cimeter is a larger knife, with around a 10-inch blade and a slightly curved tip. It is used for larger cuts. When you are cutting steaks, chops, or larger muscles, the extra size comes in handy. Expect to spend around $40 to 50 or more for a high-quality cimeter knife.

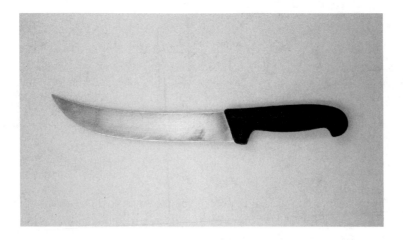

Cleaver

The star in horror movies, the cleaver is easy to use and relatively inexpensive. Even with modern power tools, the old-fashioned cleaver is hard to pass up for getting the job done.

For the home butcher, the cleaver is used in a great number of jobs. For example, the cleaver is needed when more force is required, such as with pork chops, or other larger cuts. Expect to spend around $50 for a high-quality cleaver with a strong blade of good, sturdy weight.

Bone Saw

The bone saw is used to cut through bone, thick tendon, and joints at the cuts when deboning isn't an option. This is one tool in particular that needs to be a really high quality. Pick one up from a butcher supply or high-end kitchenware store, but expect to spend over $50 for a durable saw.

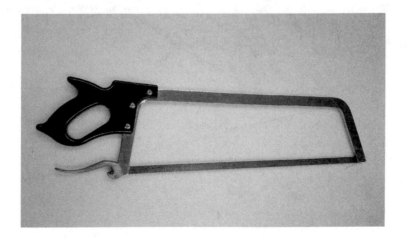

Make sure your blades are a food-grade metal and designed for butchering use. The handle should be strong, durable, easy to clean and easy to change out the blades when a new one is needed.

Breaking Hook

A breaking hook is often called a boning hook. This isn't related to Captain Hook's pirate hook, but rather is used to aid in the overall butchering process.

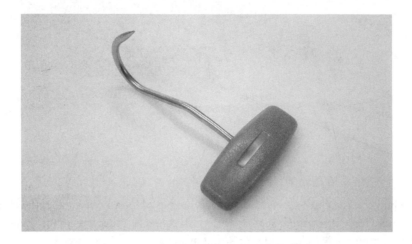

The plastic or aluminum handle can be held in your hand, while the metal hook allows you to peel away muscles. The extra leverage you gain with the hook makes it easier to separate the large pieces. At only about $10, this is a tool you can easily afford to keep on hand.

Sharpening Stone

A sharpening stone is used to sharpen your butcher knives. There are several types of stones with various sizes of grit. It's helpful to have at least two stones with differing sizes of grit to help create the best edge. A medium-coarse stone will run in the range of 1,000x, while a medium-fine stone will be closer to 4,000x.

Oil or water can be used to lubricate the stone. If you use water, soak the stone for about 10 minutes before using. Oil can be applied directly to the stone just prior to sharpening your knives. Water is easier to clean however, so it's just a matter of preference. Expect to spend around $50 for a combination stone or as much was $75 or more a single stone. They should last indefinitely.

BUTCHER'S TIP

To sharpen a knife, place it on a lubricated stone at a 20-degree angle and work the knife from tip to heel in a circular motion. Repeat each side until you've created a burr or slight curl in the metal at the edge. Once you've sharpened the knife and there is a small burr, use the finest stone to remove the burr, keeping the same 20-degree angle as before.

You'll only need the lightest pressure as you are trying to remove the burr only; hard pressure will create a new burr. You will know the knife is sharp enough when you use it on the meat. You can further hone the blade with the honing steel as you work.

Honing Steel

A honing steel is used to maintain the knife's sharp edge as you work. A knife blade may begin to dull during the process of butchering, so honing the blade with a steel will keep things moving quickly.

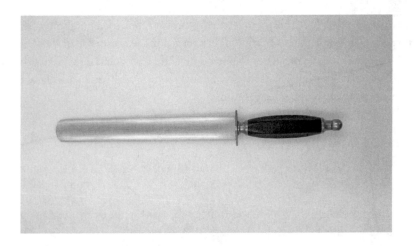

You don't just rub a knife along the steel willy-nilly—you have to use the same 20-degree angle you use when sharpening your knife. And you only need to swipe the blade over it a couple times to hone the edge. A high-quality steel will cost anywhere from $20 to over $100.

Butcher's Twine

Butchering twine is used to truss up a bird or to secure prime rib bones. It has to be strong enough to not break with use. Expect to spend about $10 a roll on a good quality twine such as 16-ply cotton twine.

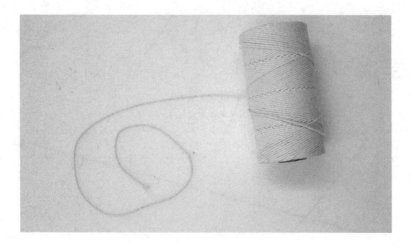

Tabletop Grinder

A meat grinder is one of the more costly investments upfront, but it's a good one. Being able to grind your own meat at home means better quality meat for a less expensive price. Beyond that, it also means that trimmings of meat from your homemade cuts that would have otherwise been wasted are used. A tabletop grinder will be easy enough to use, and you can usually find sausage nozzle attachments to easily make sausages, too.

Miscellaneous Items

There are smaller items you'll want to have on hand to make it easier to finish your butchering process:

- Towels are always nice to have on hand to keep the workspace clean or to use as a grip if your hand is slipping while butchering.

- A block scraper will clean the cutting board surface by removing oily fat buildup.

- A bone scraper is used to remove any loose bits of bone dust after sawing through bones to create your premium cuts.

- Your trussing needle is used to tie the backs of birds together after you've stuffed them or to tie a pork roast with skin still on the muscle.

- Keep a mechanical scale nearby for peace of mind when making individual cuts of meat or adding spices to sausages and making precise measurements.

The Extra Stuff

As with any hobby or job, there are tools that are the bare minimum and tools that make everything easier. Here are a few of the nice-to-haves if your budget allows:

Band saws make a variety of cuts easier, for example, cutting straight chops or making stock bones easier to manage. Cuts are easier, less messy, and faster.

A *vacuum pack machine* will extend the freezer life of meat up to 6 months beyond freezer paper. It also provides visibility while digging through all those cuts.

BUTCHER'S TIP

Butchering doesn't finish with making the cuts—you have to have a way to preserve the meat in the freezer. Many home butchers will use butcher paper that allows you to wrap the cuts and mark on the paper what is inside (as well as the date). The other option is a vacuum seal with freezer plastic that removes all the air and usually results in a fresher taste after long-term storage. The vacuum method, however, is more expensive to get started with and requires a label for marking the cuts and dates on the outside.

For cutting beef, a *roll bar* or rail helps by suspending the carcass and allowing you to use gravity while seeming out larger muscles. These are used in packing houses and would rarely be seen in the homestead. Perhaps a contraption affixed to a tractor bucket could suffice in order to hang a hook in a barn or garage.

The Breakdowns 2

This part is the nitty gritty of how to work with the individual animals a home butcher might want: beef, lamb (and goats or deer), pork, poultry, rabbit, and fish. Follow along with step-by-step pictures to help you learn the basics and develop your skills as a home butcher so you can create personalized cuts for your family without boutique prices.

Beef   ❧   3

The largest of the meat animals discussed in this book, beef is the meat produced from cattle, usually a steer or unbred heifer. While there are smaller, miniature breeds becoming more popular on small backyard farms, the most common cattle are large and can produce hundreds of pounds of meat from a single animal. For this reason a home butcher may prefer to source a side of beef (one half) instead of the full cow. Either way, beef is one of the most popular meats in the United States and Canada, and is prized as a juicy, flavorful red meat.

Introducing the Animal

Cattle are usually grown to a butchering weight of around 1,200 to 1,500 pounds live weight (the weight of the animal before slaughtering). The slaughter process takes the animal down to what is called the *hanging weight,* where the carcass is skinned, gutted, and then cut into two halves. The hanging weight is usually about 60 percent of the live weight, so this brings your total poundage down to about 720 to 900 pounds.

There is a difference in the quality of meat of grain-finished or grain-fed beef and the meat you'll see on grass-finished beef. Cuts from beef that is grass-finished or 100-percent grass fed will have less marbling throughout the cut, making the majority of the fat easy to trim away. Additionally, the fat itself has higher levels of omega-3 and much higher levels of conjugated linoleic acid (CLA), the nutrient that that is associated with lowering the risk of heart disease. In fact, the end cuts are much lower in fat as well: a 6-ounce steak from a grass-finished steer will be 100 calories less than a similar sized steak from a grain-fed steer.

As a result of the leaner, more even composition, meat from a grass-finished steer will need to be cooked with more care and attention. Think lower (heat) and slower (cook times), and you'll be on the right track (which of course means more amazing and rich flavor).

DEFINITION

The **hanging weight** is the weight of the carcass after evisceration.

The Main Breakdown

With beef, you often source the animal already cut into more manageable sections, halved and then split at the rib and the loin. We will walk you through the process of creating the individual cuts from that assumption. This gives you five main sections (hindquarter, boning out the hip, the loin, ribs, and beef chuck) already broken down from the start—a good place to begin your home butchery work.

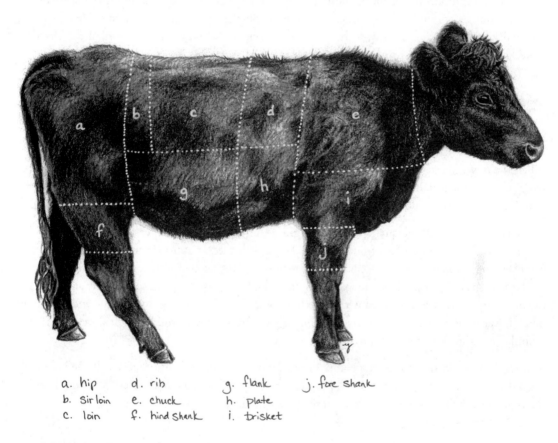

a. hip   d. rib   g. flank   j. fore shank
b. sirloin   e. chuck   h. plate
c. loin   f. hind shank   i. brisket

BUTCHER'S TIP

In Chapter 4, we demonstrate breaking down the full lamb carcass into main sections before working up the individual cuts. In Chapter 5, you see a side of pork, which is one side of the animal (either the full left or full right side).

Hindquarter

Working with the hindquarter is when using the breaking hook will really come in handy (see the section "The Essential Tools" in Chapter 2 for a picture of a breaking hook).

Peel off the flank steak.

To clean up the hindquarter of beef before processing the individual cuts, you can first peel off the flank steak.

Insert breaking hook here

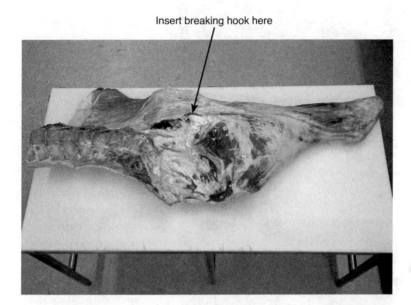

1. Start with the hind-quarter turned up. In this primal cut we will be breaking down the flank, sirloin, and hip of beef.

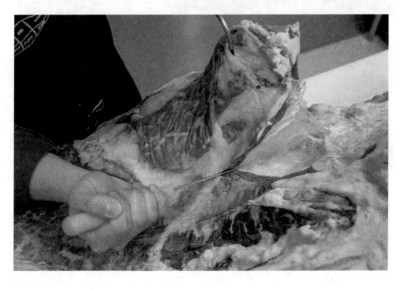

2. Lift the flank steak up and get ready to make your cut. Cut starting from where it meets the hip of beef area and stay as close to the sirloin (back) as possible. Cut the entire flank section apart from the hindquarter.

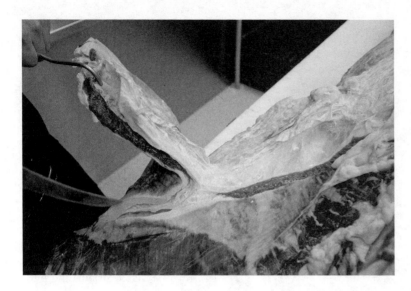

3. Cut all the way down the length of the belly to remove the flank steak, using the breaking hook for support as needed.

Separate the hip from the loin.

Next we'll be removing the loin, long loin (sirloin) and whole loin cuts all the way down. This will separate the hip from the loin.

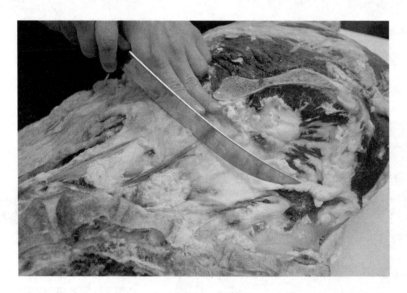

1. Measure about two fingers from the aitchbone. Find your place to cut the loins from the hindquarter and score the line with your long knife.

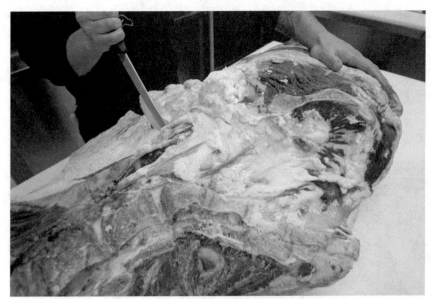

2. Make the cut square to the long loin and cut deep, until you reach bone. You will need to use a good force to get through all the meat with your big butchering knife, but it will prevent you from cutting any of the meat with the saw.

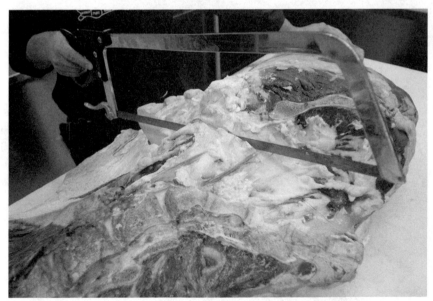

3. Use the bone saw to cut through the bone only, and switch back to the knife to finish the separation. Switching to your knife to finish the separation will prevent tearing of the meat.

Boning Out the Hip

Removing the bone from the hip will be a chore, but it will provide a variety of boneless roasts. The bones can be used for stock, dog food, etc.

Remove the spider steak.

First we'll be removing the spider steak from the top of the hip area. In beef, the spider steak is large enough to slice up for a quick-fry steak, such as sandwich slices, fajitas, or salad toppings.

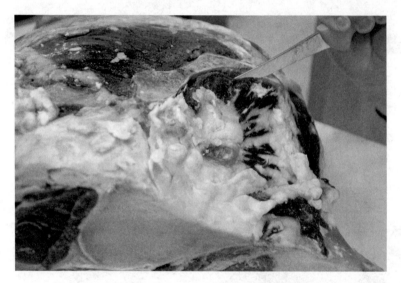

1. Find the curved bone with the tip of your knife and carefully peel out the whole muscle. Work the knife tip under the spider steak and stay as close to the bone as possible and preserve the largest amount of meat.

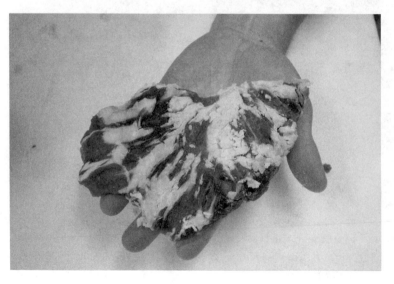

2. Once you remove the spider steak, it should be about the size of your hand. It is the perfect size for a quick meal and is an easy-to-cook steak.

Remove the aitchbone.

Now that you've removed the spider steak, the aitchbone is exposed for easier removal.

1. Score the inside of the socket area with the knife to sever the bone's attachments to the meat there. This will also begin the process of cutting the aitchbone free from the hip.

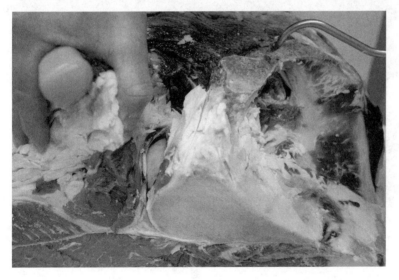

2. Use your breaking hook as needed to help give you leverage up underneath the aitchbone. With the other hand, use the tip of the knife to cut the meat from the underside of the bone.

3. Sever the tendon at the top of the femur to free the aitchbone. This will also expose the ball and socket. Note the unusual shapes and angles of the aitchbone that take care to work around.

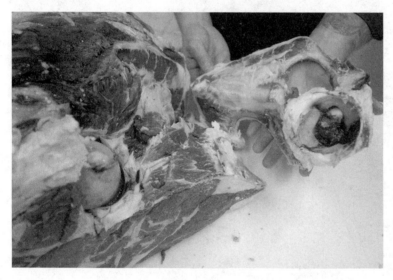

4. Use the tip of the knife and stay *hard on the bone* so you don't ruin the meat while removing the large aitchbone. It takes some effort, but continue to cut the meat away from the bone until you've freed the aitchbone completely.

DEFINITION

When butchering, **hard on the bone** refers to keeping your knife as close to the bone as possible.

Remove the shank bone.

Next we will remove the shank bone to free the hip of beef.

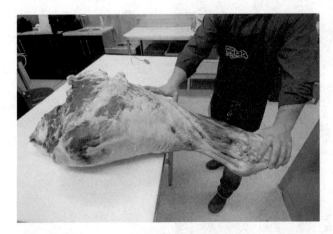

1. Move the meat to the edge of the table or counter so you can get good leverage.

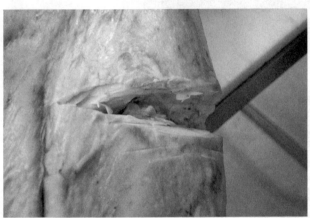

2. Find the bend in the front of the joint and use your knife to free the joint by cutting through the soft tissues of meat and tendon.

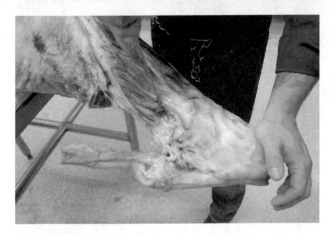

3. Before fully removing the shank, cut the Achilles' tendon so you can bone out the shank.

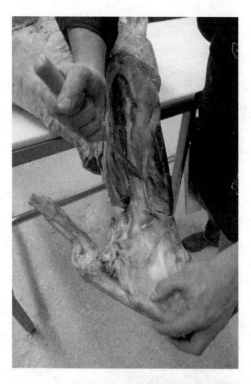

4. Work with the knife to cut toward the joint and separate the meat from the bone, working as close to the bone as possible. Cut the meat free from the bone, working from the heel toward the hip.

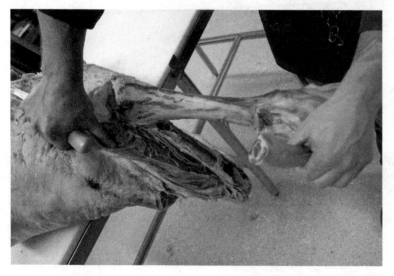

5. Work the bone free from the socket and use your knife to cut the knee joint free so you can remove the shank bone and Achilles' tendon completely.

Remove the femur bone.

Now we will be removing the femur bone from the hip of beef to finish the boning out process.

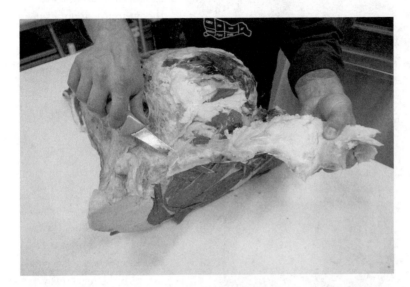

1. Clean up the thick layers of fat on the exterior of the hip so you can clearly see the seams of the muscles.

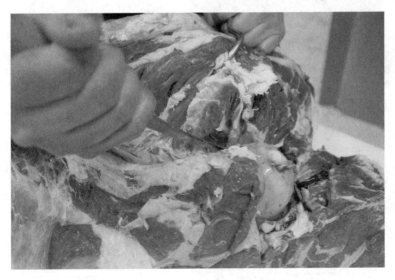

2. Next we will be separating the inside round and the sirloin tip and exposing the femur bone. You want to separate on the natural seams of the muscles. Work the seam just on the outside of the femur bone with your knife. Use your breaking hook to pull open the meat until you reach the bone.

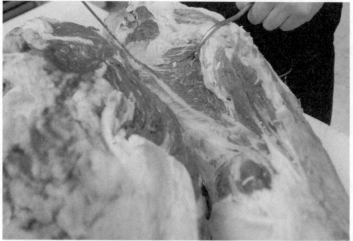

3. Now work hard on the bone of the femur along its length, pulling back the meat as you go. Using the tip of the knife and working in small, close cuts will preserve the meat as much as possible.

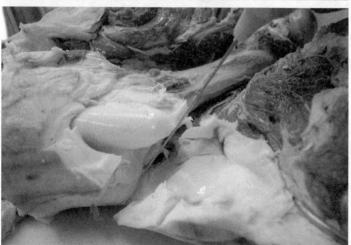

4. Once you've freed one side of the femur bone, turn (not flip) the hip of beef for better leverage so you can pull the meat away from the other side of the femur. You're still working on the top side of the hindquarter, but you now have a better angle.

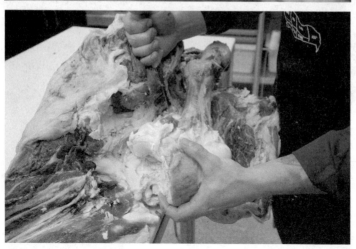

5. Move the hip to the edge of the table or counter so you can bend it open on the edge. This will allow you to roll the bone open and work up underneath the bone more easily with your knife. Work carefully around the ends of the bones, as both joints will need extra knife work to free up.

6. Pull the bone free as you are able, and finish freeing up the knuckle side of the bone to completely detach it. Notice how the meat is falling open along the edge of the table, making it easier to work the bone free.

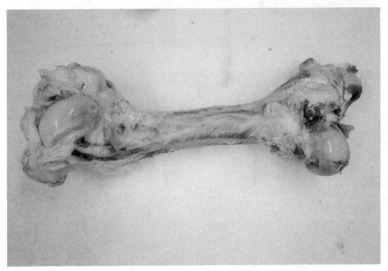

7. The completely freed femur bone makes a great bone for barrel bones, stock bones, or for your dog.

WARNING

Don't be surprised if the joints have a lot of slippery fluid—you will want to have a firm grasp on the bone!

Peel open the leg of beef.

Now you will peel open the leg of beef so you can carve out the rounds and other steaks and roasts.

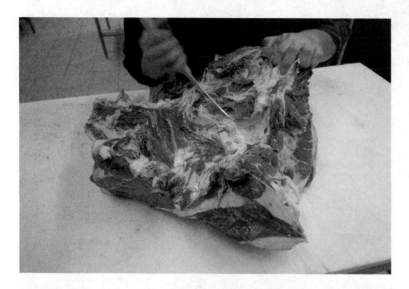

1. Locate the natural seam that will separate the inside round from the eye of round steak and trim up any excess fat you might find. Work with your knife tip to open up the natural seam between the inside round and eye of round, applying steady pressure with your hand to work it open.

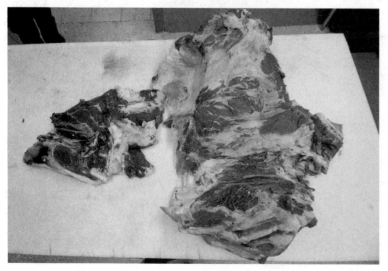

2. Remove the heel. The boneless heel meat is most suited for grinding, so it's a less premium cut compared to the steaks you uncover below it. Try not to score the more premium cuts underneath.

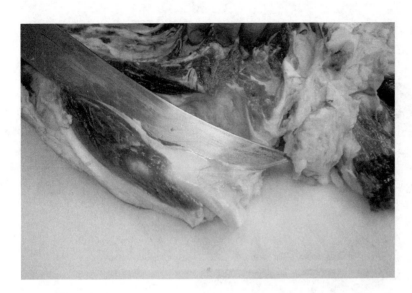

3. Remove the two thick tendons from the heel meat before you cut it into chunks for your home grinder.

BUTCHER'S TIP

Some grinders can handle larger chunks of meat, but some home grinders need the meat cut into smaller squares. Make sure to cut the meat destined for ground meat into whichever size is appropriate for your model meat grinder.

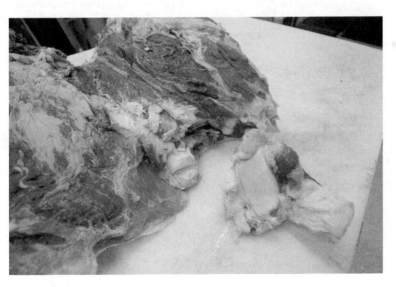

4. The knuckle bone is the last boney piece to remove, so carefully cut it out and discard, again, staying close against the bone as you work.

Remove the sirloin tip.

Next we will be removing the sirloin tip from the rest of the meat.

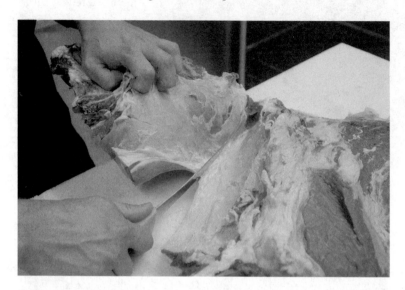

1. Locate the natural seam and work the sirloin tip free, using the knife as necessary.

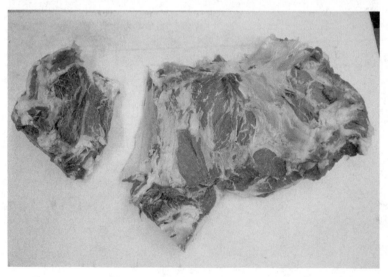

2. Work gently along the natural seam and remove the sirloin tip from the inside round. Set it aside to finish working it up later (see the section "Work loose the sirloin tip steaks").

Work apart the hip meat.

Now we will be working apart all the delicious roasts and steaks from the hip meat that is left.

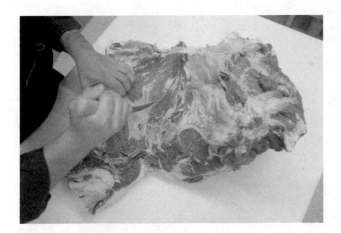

1. Remove the outside round by continuing to work along the natural seams of the muscle. Use your knife as necessary to cut through the fascia and completely remove the large muscle.

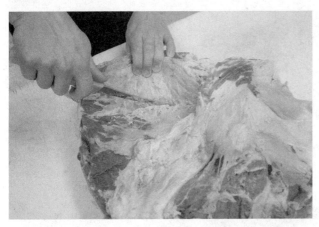

2. Open the seam exposed after removing the outside round to expose the eye of round.

3. Cut the eye of round free by pulling it along the seams.

A CUT ABOVE

You can simply trim the fat from around the eye of round cut and tie it up as an individual piece if you want to increase the number of roasts you get from your steer. It's a simple way to prepare the cut for a lean, healthy dinner option. As with the inside round roasts, you can tie a strip of pork fat on the top to help keep the roast from getting too dry. Another preparation for eye of round, also known as bresaola, is that it be salted and dry cured.

Remove the interior leg vein.

Now we have the inside round and need to remove a large interior vein from inside the leg. It's not a good idea to leave the vein inside the meat. It will alter the taste, and it isn't an edible part of the meat, so taking the time now to remove it is beneficial.

1. Locate the vein inside the muscle of the leg so you can remove it.

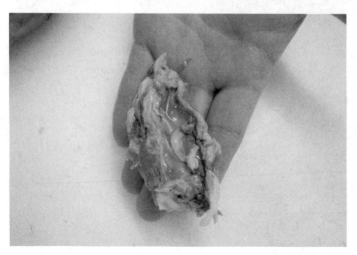

2. Remove the vein by cutting it free with the tip of your knife and discard it, as it won't be used for anything edible.

Clean up the interior inside round.

Clean up the inside of the inside round by trimming away all the extra fat. You'll do this on the exterior side in the section that follows.

1. Clean all the fat off the inside round.

2. If your meat has hung for aging, then you will have a dark spot on the outside of the inside round from exposure to the elements (more like a scab). That part should be cut out completely and discarded. Remove the scarred meat from the other side of the inside round.

A CUT ABOVE

Inside round, also known as top round, is a lean cut of meat that is lower in calories than some of the fattier cuts. Many people prefer to marinate it because the leaner fat content can make for a drier flavor otherwise. It's perfect for slow, moist cooking like a slow-cooker roast or oven-roast. Other times you can marinate it and slice it into thinner slices for sandwiches and fajitas.

Clean up the exterior inside round.

When you trim the fat from the exterior side of the inside round steak, you'll expose a natural seam that makes it easy to make this last cut.

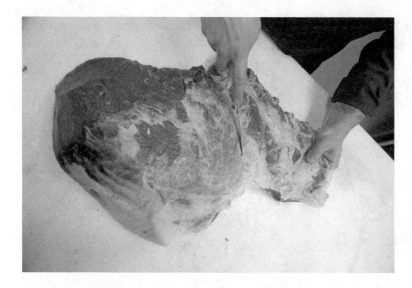

1. Open the seam to remove the cap muscle.

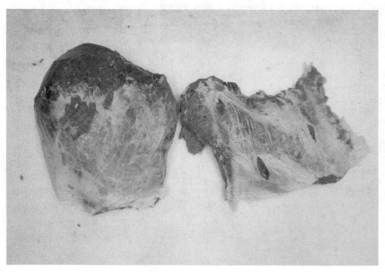

2. Pull the whole muscle off the top of the inside round; this is known as removing the cap. The cap portion is used for ground meat, while the beautiful, solid inside round steak makes an excellent lean meal.

3. Trim all the excess fat off the inside round to prepare it for cooking. The excess fat can be used as trimmings for grinding.

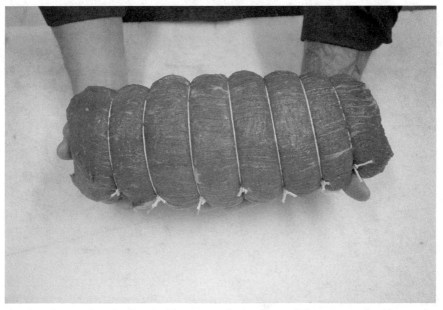

4. Cut the inside round in half going with the fiber of the meat so you have two meal-sized portions to use. The individual roasts can be tied, or you can tie a strip of fat over the top to add flavor and juice during cooking.

Break up steaks from the outside round.

Returning to the outside round cut that was separated earlier, there are a couple steaks to break up.

1. Open the top muscle along the seam, using your hands and knife as needed. Cut the excess fat off the top. If some meat is still attached, that is okay because it will go in with trimmings for grinding. The fatty muscle becomes ground meat, as it's not a suitable size for a steak.

2. The outside round is then cleaned of excess fat, especially from the exterior edges. Use your knife to make a small incision and work along the length to fully remove the silver "skin" or membrane. Clean up any of the other external fat as needed to prepare the outside round.

3. Cut the meat into chunks or cubes for stew meat by cutting into 1- to 2-inch slices against the grain and then cubing the slices for stews.

A CUT ABOVE

The outside round makes excellent roast beef and is a common cut for the deli slices of roast beef you might purchase in the store.

Work loose the sirloin tip steaks.

Coming back to the sirloin tip, we will be peeling off the top cap muscle and then working loose all the other steaks using the natural seams.

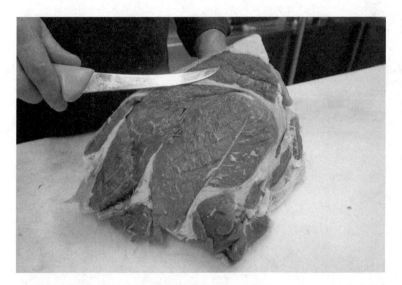

1. Find the exposed seam and begin working the top muscle loose. The top muscle (where the knife tip is pointing in the photo) is the cap muscle you'll work loose first for ground meat.

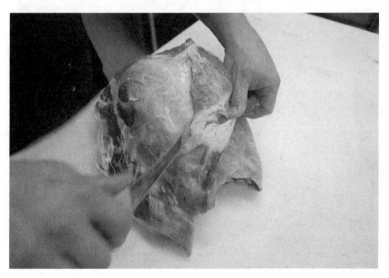

2. Use the tip of the knife to work the seam without scoring the meat too much. Now the side muscle will be removed along the natural seam. This cut is usually used for ground meat and stew meat, so you'll chunk the portions that are meaty and put the fatty bits into the trim bucket for grinding.

3. The sirloin tip section will also have a silver skin membrane to clear off. Remove the thick silver skin (membrane) from the other side of the sirloin tip.

4. Any exterior, tough fat can be removed at this time until you have a finished, clean roast ready to cook.

5. The roast can be tied with a strip of pork fat on top to naturally baste during the roasting process.

A CUT ABOVE

Sirloin tip roast is considered one of the more tender roasts from the hip, but is still maintains a leaner composition than many of the steaks. It is lean, nutritious, and considered a higher value roast.

Trim up the flank steak.

We originally removed the flank from the hip of beef in the section "Peel off the flank steak." Now we'll trim it up and prepare the flank steak while adding lots of trimming to our ground meat bucket.

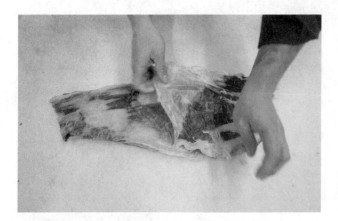

1. Peel the membrane away from the flank by working it loose at one end.

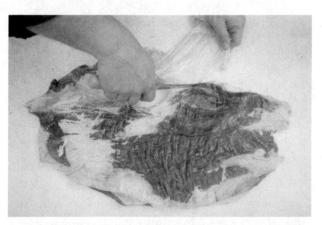

2. Use your knife to cut the membrane off the edge of the flank. The membrane can be added to ground meat. The flank steak is visible in the area that would be left if you cut away the fattiest meat portions.

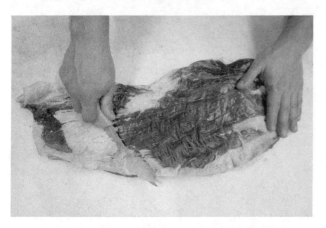

3. Cut out the rounded flank steak by removing the fatty, uneven end.

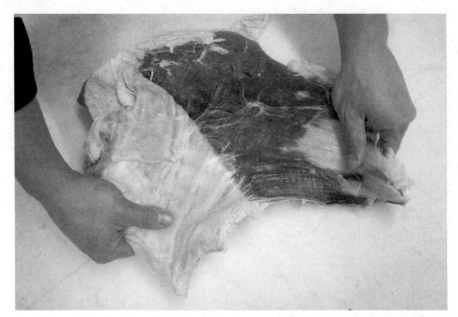

4. Flip over the flank steak and pull again to remove the membrane and excess fat.

A CUT ABOVE

The flank steak is often a favorite cut, popular in fajitas and on salads, and is known to be juicy and flavorful.

The Loin

The loin section has several tender cuts, including many steaks, such as the bavette, the sirloin, tri-tip, strip steaks, tenderloins or porterhouse, and T-bone steaks. These are premium and valuable cuts, so work carefully to preserve the best quality meat possible!

Remove the bavette steak.

First we will remove the bavette steak, also called the sirloin flap, or minute steak. This is a cut not usually available in the grocery store, but is an excellent, chewy steak usually served medium rare after cooking for just a few short minutes.

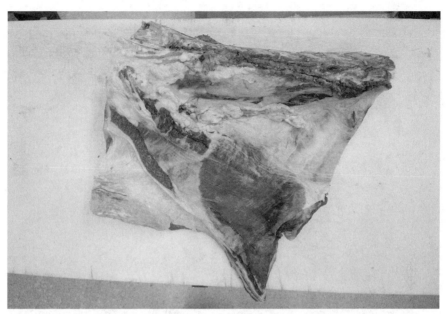

1. The loin section consists of the tender meat between the hip and the ribs from the back to belly of the cow.

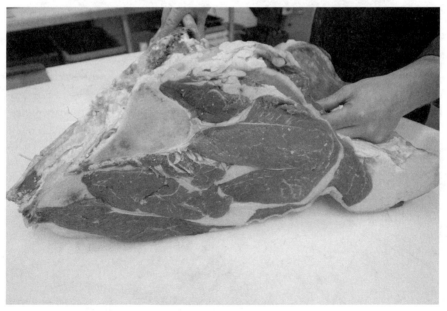

2. Locate the seam where we will begin to work the bavette loose.

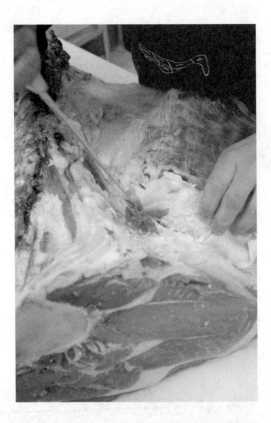

3. Pull the bavette up from the tenderloin below it until you've reached the end of the tenderloin.

4. Now you can finish the bavette with a cut between the eye and tail end of the New York strip. See the mark of where to cut in the photo.

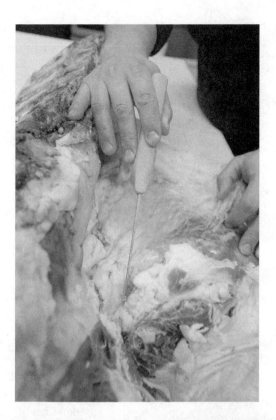

5. Score the cut lightly at first so you have a clear line to follow. Bend the flap over the table to open it up, and cut carefully along the line until you reach the line of fat under the bavette that will allow you to remove the bavette from the rest of the loin.

6. Work along the scored cut until you reach the natural seam underneath. This line of fat is a natural seam that allows you to remove the bavette without damaging the rest of the premium cuts in the loin section. It's a tricky cut, so just watch out when cutting into the scored mark and you'll be good.

7. Pull the bavette apart from the loin carefully.

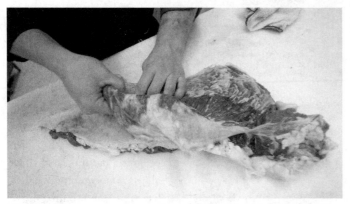

8. As with other cuts, remove the membrane and fatty bits from the top of the bavette. Trim the steak a little bit, but don't cut off all the meat.

9. Now the bavette is trimmed and ready to cut into usable sections.

A CUT ABOVE

The bavette is an amazing steak for the grill, panfried, or sliced across the grain and cooked quickly for tender steak strips.

Remove the meat from the skirt.

Next we will be removing the meat from the skirt of the loin where the bavette had been resting. This meat can simply be used for grinding or chunked for stew, as it's not particularly tender or flavorful.

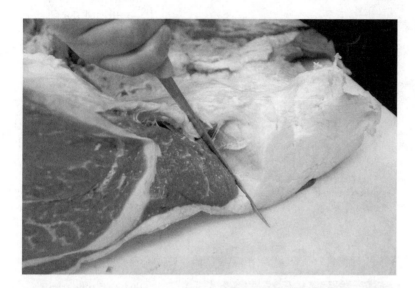

1. Find the natural seam from just outside the sirloin.

2. Cut the meat right along that line all the way to the last rib.

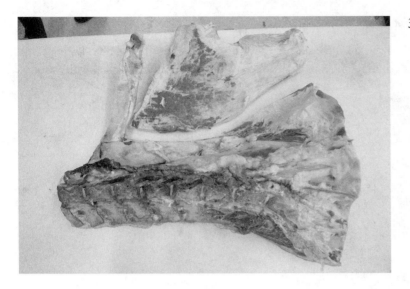

3. Cut the meat completely off the loin. You can cut the meat into usable sections and discard the fat.

Remove the tenderloin.

Now we will turn our attention to the tenderloin.

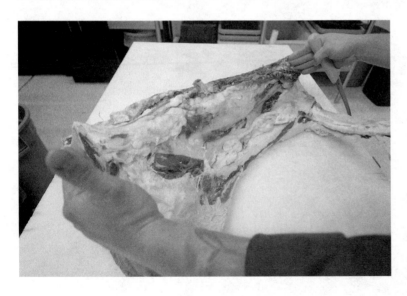

1. The beef tenderloin runs the entire length of the loin, so we will be removing it as a single muscle first.

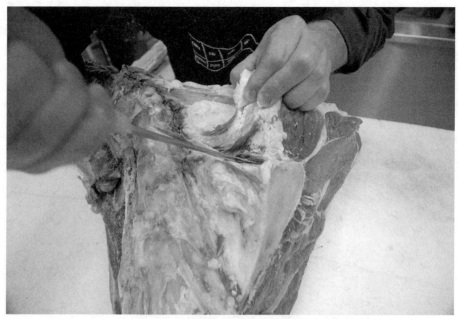

2. Use the tip of the knife to work around the bone and free the meat from the cradle of the bone.

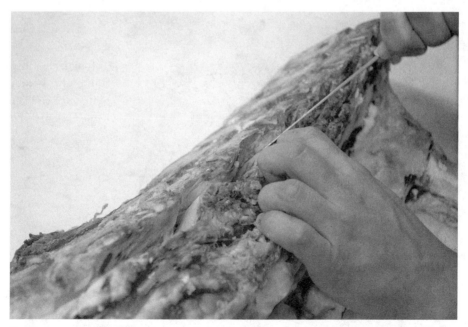

3. Once you've freed about the top couple inches of the meat, come to the other end of the loin and free the meat from the divets of the spine.

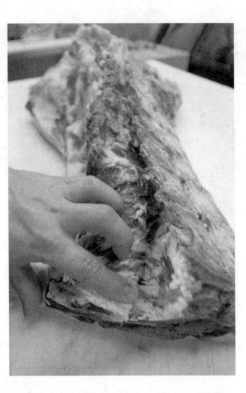

4. Work around each of the crevices carefully, staying right up against the bone.

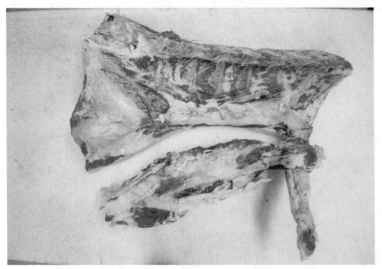

5. Scoop out to free the tenderloin, working as close to the ribs, spine, and other bones as possible to free the meat in one large strip.

BUTCHER'S TIP

At the butt-end of the loin, there are some odd shaped bones. Work as carefully with your knife as possible, but expect that small bits may not look picture perfect.

Clean and prepare the tenderloin.

The tenderloin is completely removed from the loin and will need to be cleaned and prepared in individual cuts.

1. Remove the heavy fat from around the tenderloin.

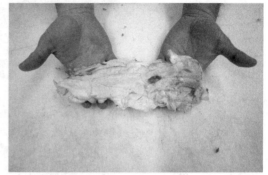

2. The fat from around the tenderloin is some of the highest quality fat on the entire cow. If you plan to render fat from beef, this is the fat to use!

3. Remove the membrane from the tenderloin, and you will expose the seam of the side chain muscle, or *chain*.

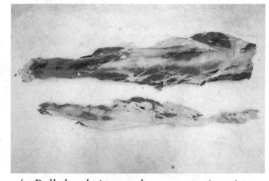

4. Pull the chain muscle to remove it, using the knife as needed in the tougher sections. This side muscle has a lot of silver skin running through it, so it isn't suitable for steaks. By removing it, you can grind it and preserve the tenderloin as a quality cut.

5. Cut away any of the heavy fat or silver skin to clean the tenderloin and finish the cut.

6. The tenderloin can now be prepared as a large roast for a large family or crowd. Alternatively, you can cut it into steak-sized pieces for individual-size cuts. That's the great thing about being a home butcher: you have all the control over what types of cuts you want and how many!

Break between the sirloin and loin.

Now we will be working out the New York strips, sirloin steaks, and more.

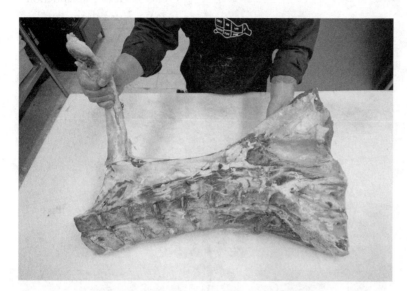

1. We will be breaking between the sirloin and the loin.

2. Cut hard with your knife between the vertebrae that curve along the spine. Pull the knife through the bone and toward the close edge. You will reach the sirloin bone as you cut, so you'll need to angle your knife to cut around the sirloin bone. If you stay as close to the bone as possible as you cut, you'll save the most meat.

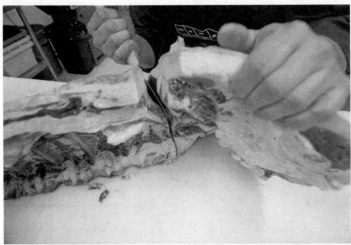

3. Flip the loin to approach it from the other side, and cut all the way to spine again. If necessary, bend it open on the edge of the table.

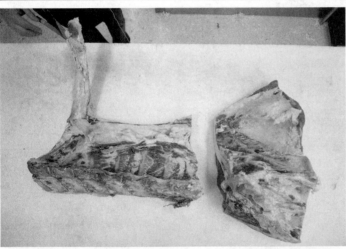

4. Use your knife to finish the cut—separating the loin from the sirloin section.

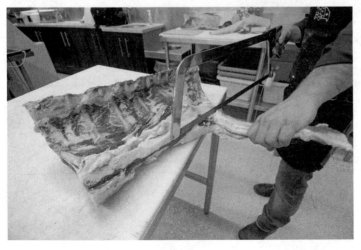

5. Use your bone saw to remove the last rib so it's not in your way while you work.

Bone out the sirloin section.

We will be boning out the sirloin section now.

1. Use the top third of your knife to follow the top bone and cut the meat. Work the tip of the knife under the bone of the sirloin and stay as close to the bone as possible.

2. Peel the bone up off the sirloin so you can continue to work it free. Stay as hard on the bone as possible until you've pulled it completely free of the sirloin.

3. Cautiously cut towards yourself so you can work up underneath the bone and all the way around. Once removed, the sirloin bone can be chopped for soup bones or dog bones.

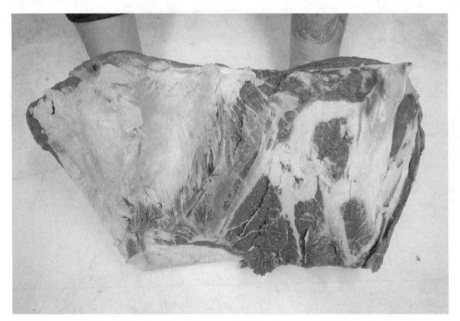

4. What you have left is the boneless top sirloin; next we will piece it into three cuts: the tri-tip, the sirloin cap, and the top sirloin steak (or roasts).

Remove the tri-tip.

Now we'll remove the tri-tip from the boneless top sirloin.

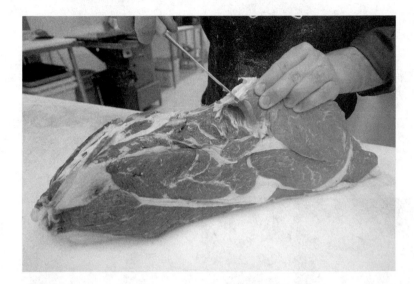

1. Begin releasing the tri-tip along the natural seam until you are about halfway through.

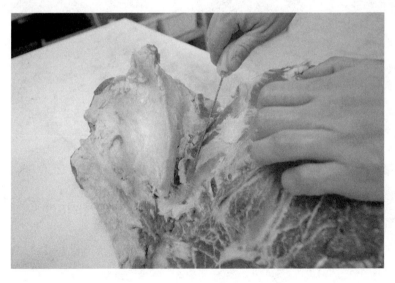

2. When you're about halfway through, make a slight cut to rediscover the seam.

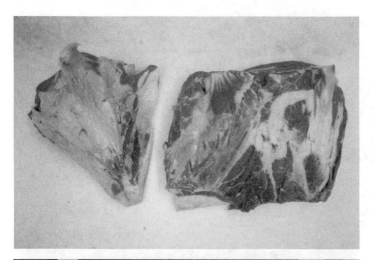

3. Make a clean cut to finish removing the tri-tip from the sirloin.

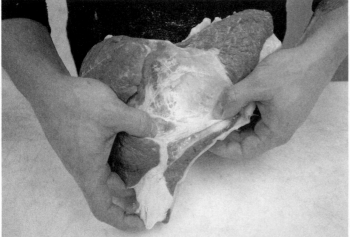

4. Pull to remove the small section of meat from underneath the tri-tip.

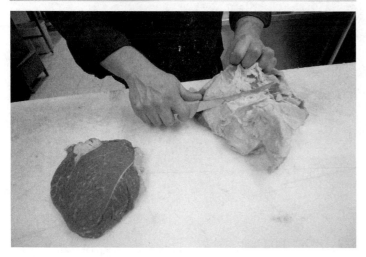

5. Clean the excess fat from the tri-tip so it's clean and ready to wrap for the freezer.

Remove the sirloin cap.

Now the sirloin cap will be removed from the sirloin. The sirloin cap is a little more tender than the tri-tip, so it's great for shish kebabs or sliced for grilling.

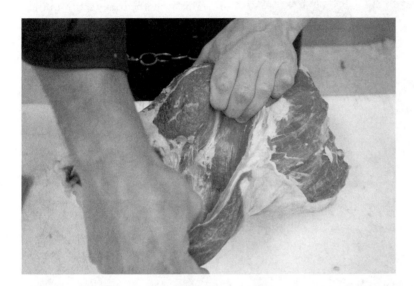

1. Work the seam open with your hands to separate the cap from the sirloin. Use your knife to encourage release as needed.

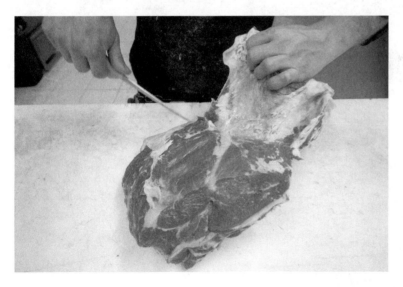

2. Peel off the cap completely so you can clean it up and store it.

Clean and finish the sirloin.

Now the sirloin can be cleaned and finished.

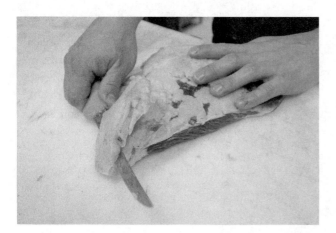

1. Trim away the heavy fat from the sirloin cap.

2. Flip it over the remove the silver skin to finish cleaning the cap.

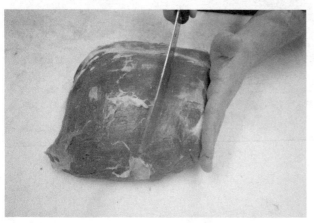

3. Slice the sirloin into nice thick steaks about $1\frac{1}{2}$ to 2 inches wide, or cut it into two sections for a good sirloin.

Bone out the loin section.

This section will show how to bone out the loin section.

1. Clean off all the excess fat from the inside of the loin so you can see the feather bones.

2. Remove the chine by cutting the tips of the ribs off the bones. (You can use a hand saw or bone saw for this.) Make sure to angle your saw to remove the chine bone. Be careful, as this saw work is tricky. A second person, with his hands holding it tight, would be of great use here.

3. To pull out the weak pin bones, sometimes you'll need to break the joints between the ribs where they attach. A simple way to do this is to use the handle end of your steal to break the attachments.

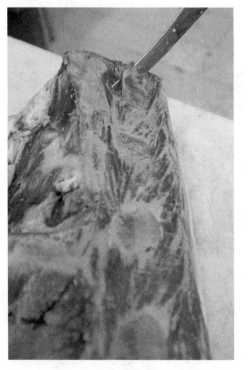

4. Carve out the pin bones and feather bones by using your knife to pry up underneath them.

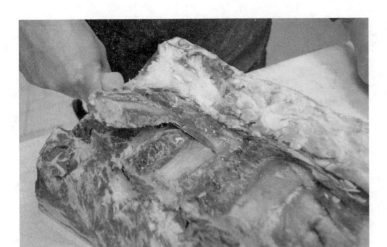

5. Now we will be removing the larger feather bones. An easy way to work them loose is to use your knife blade to lever the bones free.

6. Trim off any meat from the feather bones as you free them to add to your ground meat pile. The feather bones can then be discarded.

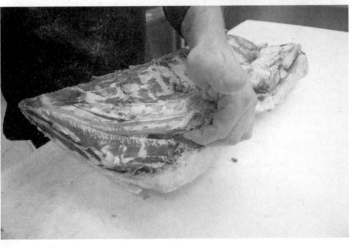

7. When you reach the last rib, you won't have any other bones to use as a lever, so you'll need to take more care in removing it. Clean off the top bone so it is exposed and you can clearly see it. Now score on each side of the bone with the tip of the knife. As always, stay close against the side of the bone.

8. Use your knife tip to scoop up and around underneath the bone. Your other hand should apply pressure by lifting the bone up. Begin peeling the bone away using steady pressure with your hand while you cut it from the meat with your knife tip. Remove and discard.

Cut the New York strip.

Now you're ready to cut your New York strip.

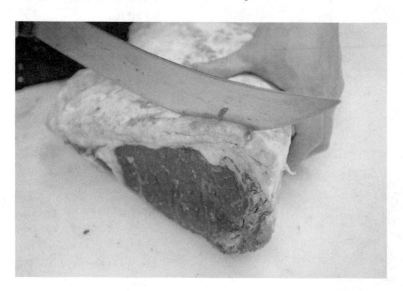

1. Remove any portions of meat darkened by dry aging. You don't want to take off too much and waste meat, so just cut the darker, scarred portion (usually around an inch or two).

2. Cut the entire length in New York strips about an inch and a quarter wide. Keep your cuts as square as possible. Clean the excess fat from the top of the strip as desired.

Ribs

The large rib section will turn into prime rib, ribs, chuck, and other cuts. It's a large section to start with, but it will become several favorite cuts for home butchers!

Separate the rib from the chuck.

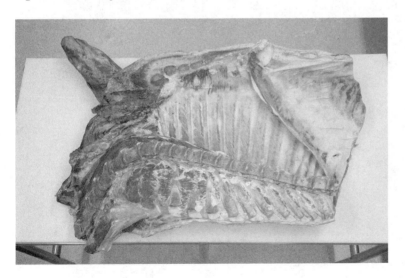

1. Count between the fourth and fifth rib to determine where you will be cutting to give you an 8-rib prime rib.

A CUT ABOVE

Some butchers prefer to cut over farther, giving you a 7-rib prime rib, but we chose to do an 8-rib prime rib. Remember it is up to you as the butcher to make the decisions on these types of cuts, and that is the beauty of home butchery—the power is yours!

2. Sink your knife straight down between the ribs and cut down the full length of the ribs until you reach resistance.

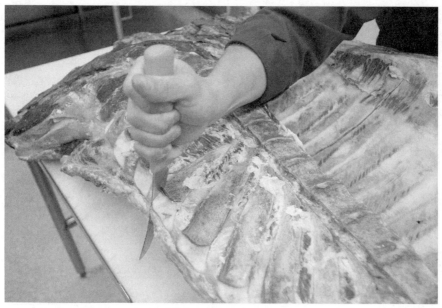

3. Make a mark at the close edge of the rib and then make a forward cut. Then mark the far edge of the rib so when you flip it over you'll see the marks where the cut should go.

4. Flip it over, and make a stronger cut through the fleshy portions using your knife. Finish the cut with your knife, cutting through the flesh, pressing it all the way to the blade bone.

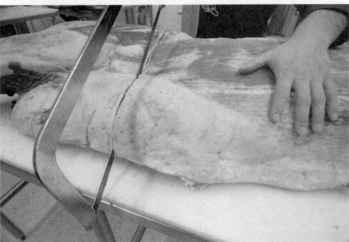

5. Use your bone saw to cut through the blade bone. You'll know when you've finished cutting the bone and reach meat again, at which point you should switch back to the knife to cut the rest of the flesh. Use the bone saw again to cut the boney attachments at the front and back side of the cut (the spine and the sterna attachment).

6. Now that you've separated the rib from the chuck, we will set aside the chuck and work up the ribs.

Remove the outside skirt steak.

We will be removing the skirt steaks from the rib now.

1. With beef, the skirt contains two steaks. There is an inside skirt (on the right) and an outside skirt (on the left) that we will be removing. We'll start with the outside skirt steak.

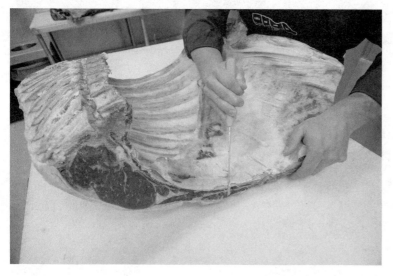

2. Cut along the natural fat line that delineates the outside skirt from the inside skirt, and make one clean cut all the way down.

3. Starting on the far edge, use your knife to finish the cut by scooping the skirt steak off the rib cage. Begin to work the outside skirt steak free from the ribs.

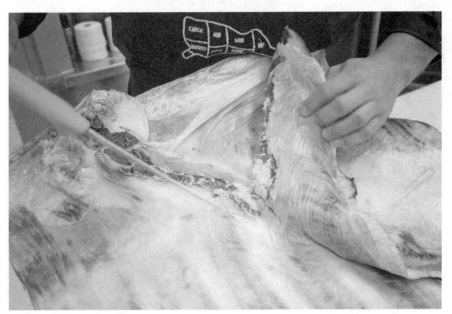

4. Keep working until you've reached your knife cut from step 2, and you'll have the outside skirt steak in one solid piece. The knife mark becomes one of the long edges of your skirt steak.

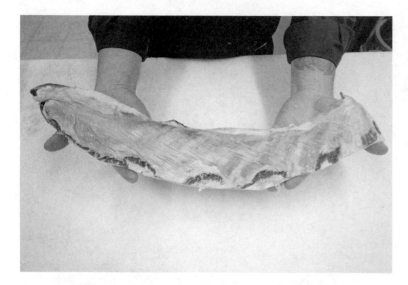

5. When fully removed, the outside skirt steak will have a thick membrane on the top that needs to be taken off.

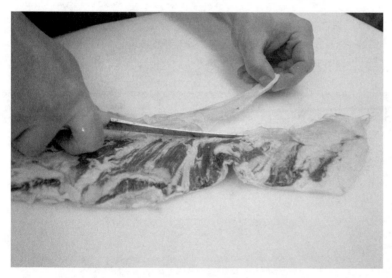

6. Peel off the thin membrane from both sides of the skirt steak, but use caution that you don't rip the skirt steak, which is a thinner and more delicate muscle.

BUTCHER'S TIP

With thinner cuts, it can be tough to remove the membranes without ripping the steak. One trick is to work the membrane free along one edge and then use the knife to cut it off at the other edge, instead of risking ripping the meat.

Remove the inside skirt steak.

With the inside skirt steak, you can peel the membrane off the first side before removing the steak.

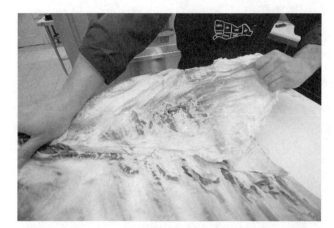

1. Peel the membrane off the inside skirt steak while it's still attached to the ribs.

2. Make two cuts to delineate the inside skirt steak—one on the inside edge of the steak and one on the outside edge of the steak.

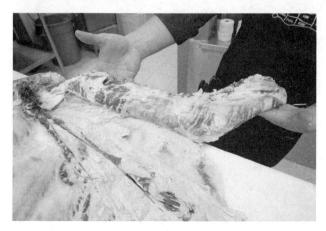

3. Use your second cut as the margin for the steak and begin to peel the skirt steak up off the ribs, working from the inside to the outside.

4. Cut the inside skirt steak off the ribs with your knife to fully remove and trim off any hanging fat pieces if needed.

Remove the plate from the ribs.

Next we will be removing the plate from the ribs.

1. Measure about four fingers width from the blade side of the ribs in, and make a knife mark on the far edge.

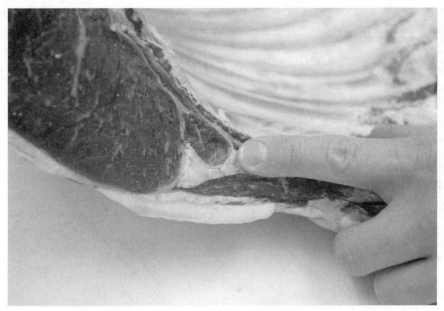

2. On the near side (the side that meets the New York strip), find the eye and measure about an inch and a half from the eye. Make a knife mark on that edge as well.

3. Make a knife mark all the way across to give yourself a clean cutting line.

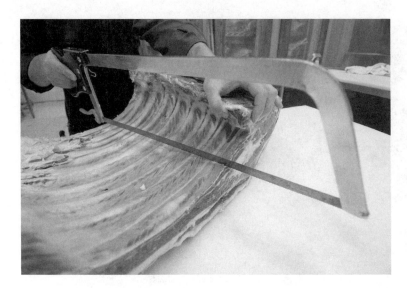

4. Use the bone saw or band saw to cut through all the bones along the cut line you made.

Work the prime rib section cap meat.

Let's work up the prime rib section now. First we will remove the cap meat, which is best used for stew meat or braising.

1. Find the blade bone on the cut side of the meat and sink your fingers into the meat to pull open the natural seam.

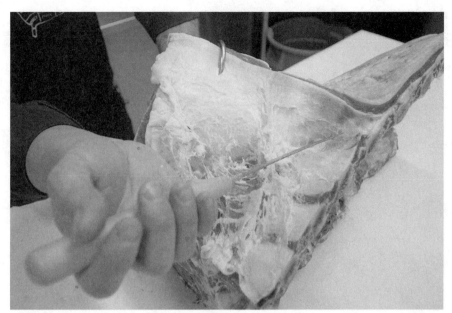

2. Use the breaking hook for leverage as needed, and pull the heavy cap meat off the prime ribs. Make easy cuts with the knife as needed to help free the cap meat.

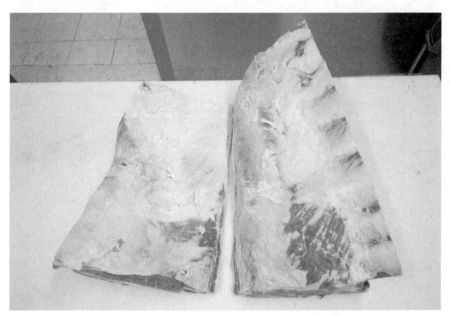

3. With the cap meat removed from the ribs, it is ready to be worked up.

4. Pull the blade bone off the cap meat now with your fingers and peel it up.

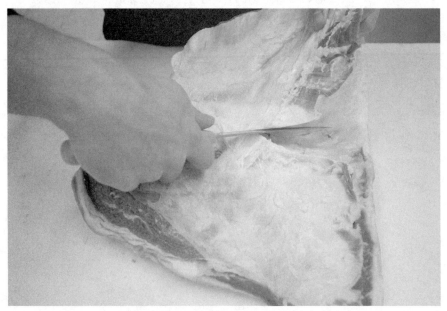

5. Use your knife to finish the cut and to prevent ripping the meat.

6. Finish boning it out with the knife by staying flat on the blade bone and cutting to remove the bone completely.

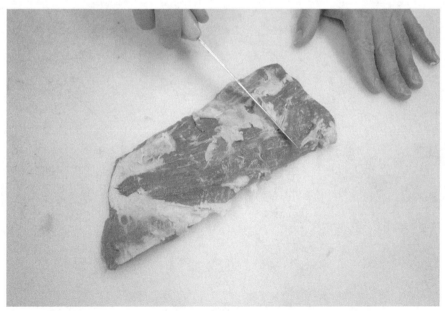

7. Clean up the excess fat from the blade meat until it's trimmed up as desired.

8. Strip it out and cube the meat for stews.

9. Cut the other piece of the cap meat in half along the natural division, to better access the two meatiest sections.

10. Clean the fat off both pieces of the cap meat so you can cut them for stew meat.

Bone out the boneless rib steaks.

Now we will be boning out the ribs for boneless rib steaks.

1. Cut off the chine bone with the bone saw (or band saw if you have access) so your ribs will be easier to work.

2. Insert the tip of the knife underneath the feather bones to loosen them; follow the cut all the way through.

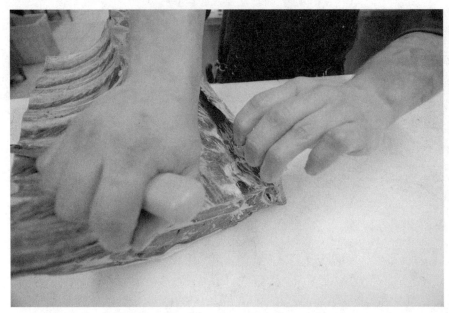

3. Peel back the feather bones and begin to work them loose.

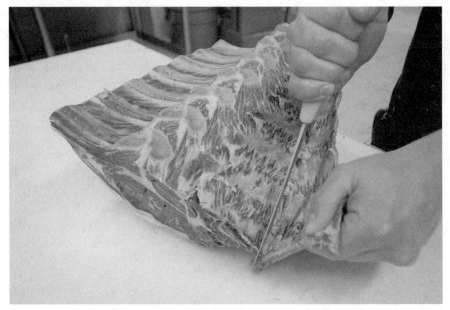

4. Cut the feather bones free to remove them.

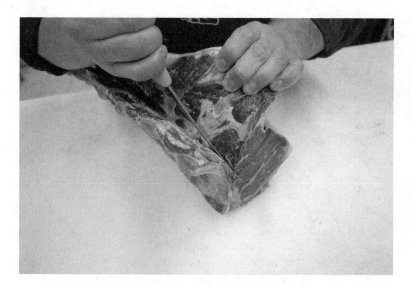

5. Remove the rib bones by staying hard on the rib as you separate the ribs from the rib eye. This will preserve as much of the rib eye meat as possible.

WARNING

While removing the rib bones, use caution to avoid cutting yourself. Do not put your hand directly on the outside of the ribs during this cut to avoid injury.

6. Continue the cut all the way through the full rack of ribs. Work the ribs loose from the meat until you are able to lay the ribs open almost completely flat.

7. Turn the ribs and cut under the ribs on the other side to finish the cut.

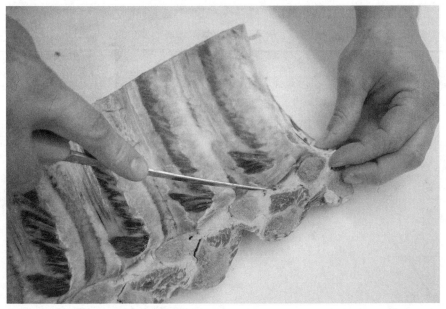

8. Remove the membrane from the top or the ribs. Score it with your knife to start it and then simply peel it off.

9. Now you have your beef ribs removed from your boneless rib meat. The rib racks can be slow cooked, braised, or cooked with your favorite rib rack recipe.

Cut the rib eye steaks.

Returning to rib eye meat, we will clean it up and finish working it out.

1. Slice off the trimmings from the end, called a lip, which can be ground up.

2. Remove the back piece, called the *back strap*.

DEFINITION

The **back strap** is the tough spinal tendons that run the length of the spine.

3. Peel back the back strap and then use your knife to cut it off.

4. Cut your rib eye steaks at the desired thickness—typically about an inch and a quarter.

5. These gorgeous steaks are high quality and usually considered one of the most desirable for their balance of texture, flavor, and fat content.

Finish the remaining rib section cuts.

Now we will finish the rib section with a few simple cuts, starting with the first three ribs for English-style short ribs.

1. Count to the fourth rib and slice with your knife into the space between the third and fourth rib. Cut all the way down the rib rack until you meet resistance.

2. Use the bone saw to finish the cut through the gristly white bone attachments.

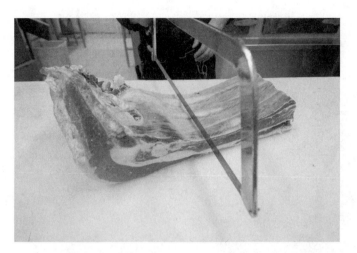

3. Cut about 8 inches down with the bone saw. This will give you the short ribs and the end of the ribs at the beginning of the brisket.

4. The brisket end can be trimmed out for stew meat and ground meat (piece on the left). The thinner end (piece on the right) is where we'll clean up our short ribs from.

5. Remove all the external fat and clean up the meat so it's well trimmed.

6. Cut between each rib to create the delicious short ribs, which are amazing braised or slow cooked.

7. The flank side of the ribs has five bones and will be simply boned out and chopped for ground meat. Use your knife to help you pry the ribs off the belly meat.

8. The belly meat can be simply rolled up with seasonings. Rolled belly roast is a popular way to eat this meat, or you can trim it out for ground beef.

Beef Chuck

The large front beef chuck is the front shoulder area, which will yield the front shank, blade roasts, flat iron steak, and a variety of soup bones. First we'll remove the foreshank.

Remove the foreshank.

To begin the process of removing the foreshank, we cut into the front leg.

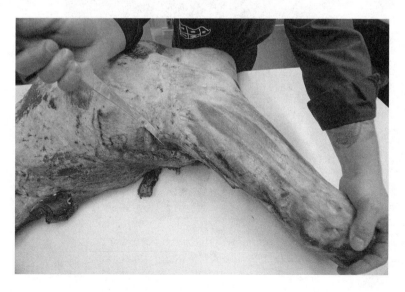

1. Sink your knife into the natural seam at the top joint. It helps if you apply downward pressure with your other hand to help open the joint.

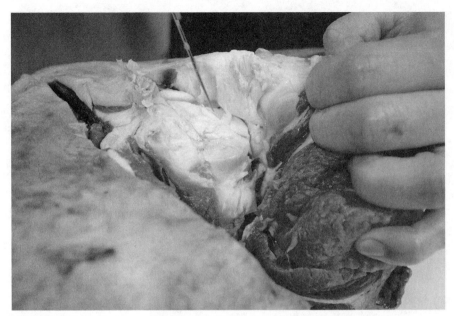

2. Use your knife to cut through the flesh and uncover the bony joint.

3. Now bend the front leg over the table or counter edge so you can work to expose the elbow joint with your knife. Use your knife to cut between the joint pieces.

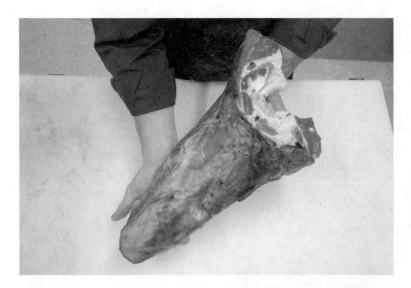

4. Finish separating the foreshank from the shoulder.

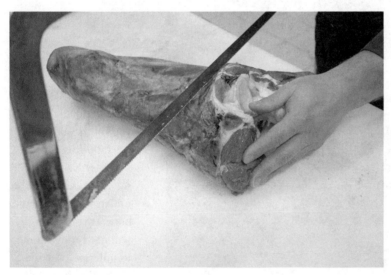

5. Square up the end of the foreshank to clean up the raw edge with your bone saw.

A CUT ABOVE

The foreshank is a cut that, while it has the potential to be tougher because the muscles were well used, is full of flavor. It can be cut into round steak-like slices or cooked as a full roast. It's perfect for stock, ground in chilies, or braised for a long time to allow the meat to soften and become more tender. Avoid dry heat and quick cooking times with this cut.

Remove the shoulder.

Now we will remove the shoulder by finding the seam that separates the arm from the brisket to preserve the muscle structure as much as possible.

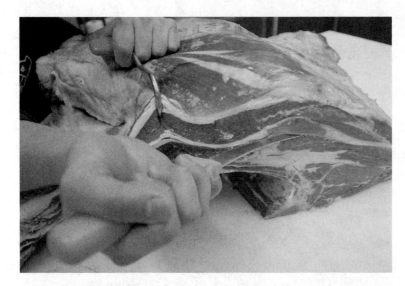

1. Work open the seam at the shoulder with your knife. You will want to use the breaking hook to help you with the heavy meat.

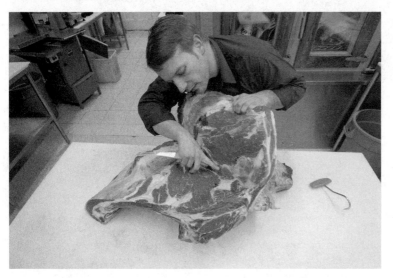

2. Work underneath the shoulder blade bone as you follow the seam. Keep pulling the shoulder blade back, staying hard along the underside of the blade bone as you cut. You will need to use force to pull open the meat of the shoulder along this seam.

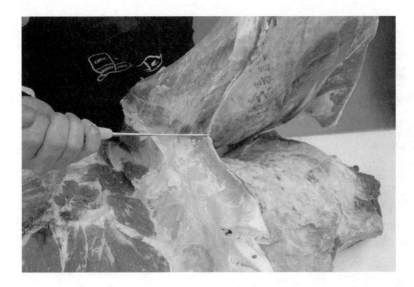

3. Stay on the outside of this muscle, the chuck tender, as you work so you can preserve that meat as you remove the shoulder. Release the shoulder with a firm cut all the way down.

A CUT ABOVE

The shoulder is a huge piece, so you end up with two very large chunks on the table. You will continue breaking them down further into usable cuts though, so don't worry!

Remove the knuckle bone.

We will be removing the knuckle bone from the chuck now.

1. Free up the top of the knuckle by cutting the meat off the bone with your knife tip. As you cut, pull the meat away from the bone with your free hand.

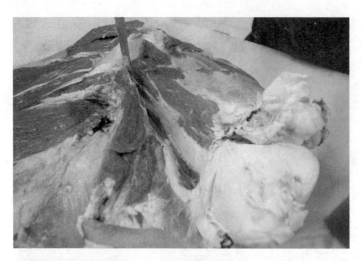

2. Cut down either side of the bone, staying hard along the bone as you work to release the meat.

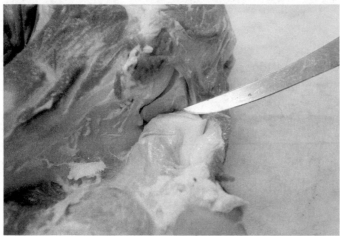

3. Cut the thick tendon toward the end of the bone. This is a harder piece to get through, so watch your knife, as you'll be pulling toward yourself here.

4. Once you've released both sides of the bone, you can begin rolling it up and over to cut it free.

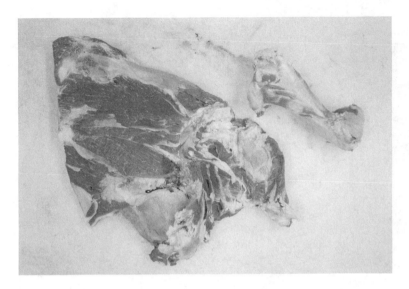

5. Remove the bone completely and set it aside to add to your beef stock or as a treat for your dog.

Remove the humerus.

Next we will be removing the humerus.

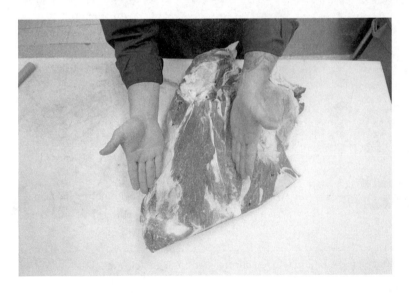

1. The paddle bone-humerus is closer to the front of the chuck. This is also known as the shoulder blade bone.

2. Start along the tiny seam on the top of the muscle and come down hard on the bone. This bone is hard enough that you shouldn't worry about going into it. Apply pressure as needed.

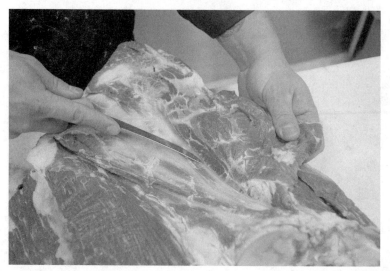

3. Clean the meat right off the bone with your knife. This extra meat from the top of the humerus is great for grinding and can be added to your trimmings bucket.

WARNING

Note that the humerus may not be the best addition to your stock pot, as it contains very little marrow.

Remove the shoulder tender.

Now we'll remove the shoulder tender.

1. The shoulder tender is great for quick grilling, stir-fry, or other dishes where tender, flavorful meat would be a boon.

2. Work along the natural seam and just peel it off. Then remove the silver skin.

Remove the chuck tender.

It's sometimes called a mock tender, or chuck tender, and can be skinned and cut into squares for stew meat. The largest section can be tied into a lovely shoulder roast.

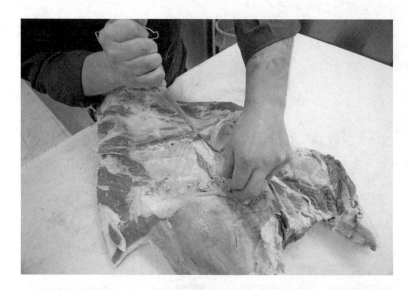

1. Cut along the blade bone to sever the attachments on the blade bone on both sides.

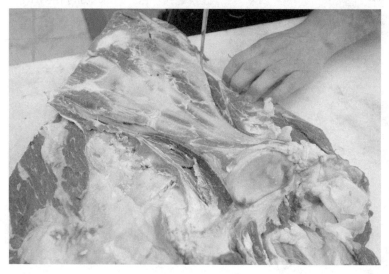

2. Make shallow cuts on both sides and then begin to work your knife underneath to lift up the shoulder bone. It helps to turn the shoulder up on the side so you can roll the muscle off the paddle bone with the help of gravity.

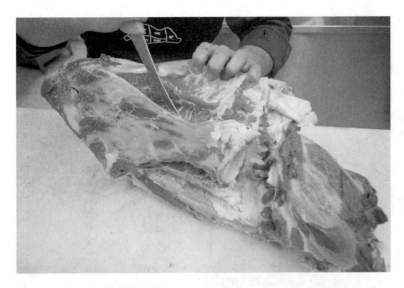

3. When you reach the end of the paddle bone, you will also be at the end of the muscle, so you can cut it off. Pull with your free hand to release the muscle.

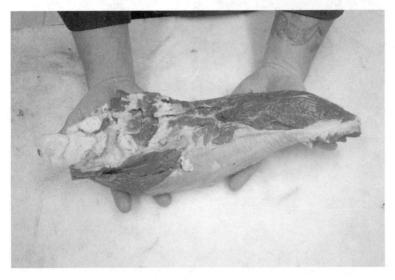

4. Remove the internal silver skin and you'll have a fantastic roasting cut.

Take out the paddle bone.

The next muscle we'll remove is the flat iron, and in order to get to it we will take out the paddle bone.

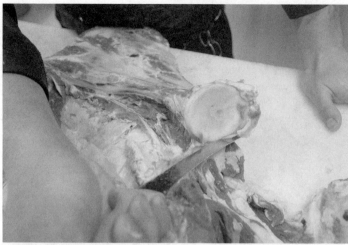

1. Work your knife just underneath the paddle bone and release the meat from under the bone. Get up and under the muscle to avoid leaving any meat on the bone.

2. Lift the bone up and away from the meat as you work, using your knife to cut as needed, so you don't rip the meat.

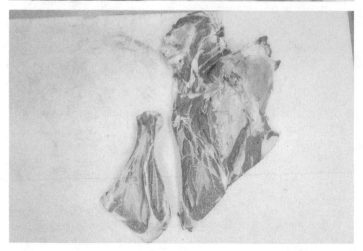

3. Work until you've completely freed the paddle bone from the flat iron muscle.

Remove the flat iron.

The muscle that was under the paddle bone is the flat iron muscle, which you'll now work free.

1. Find the natural seam previously covered by the paddle bone and begin to work it open.

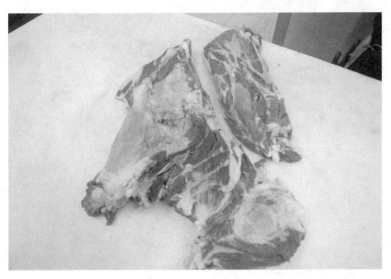

2. Cut to remove the flat iron completely. The muscle is clearly defined and ready for further clean up.

3. Peel off the membrane and fat layer from the top of the flat iron steak.

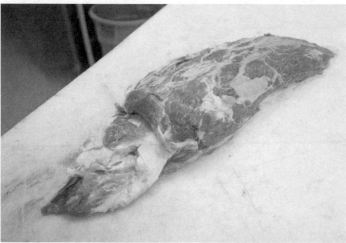

4. The flat iron is actually two flat steaks with a tendon between them. Find the tendon and carefully peel the top steak off the tendon, staying right on the tendon and silver skin of the bottom flat iron steak. This is a delicate action; go slowly and carefully. You do not want to go into the steaks.

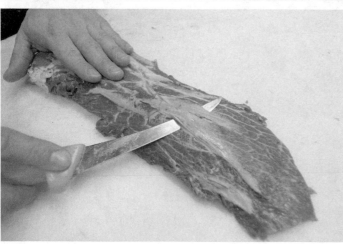

5. Trim the silver skin tissue off very carefully so you don't waste any of the delicious meat. The steaks are thin but tender.

A CUT ABOVE

The flat iron steaks may seem like a lot of work, but they are regarding as two of the most tender and desirable steaks on the entire cow.

Remove the clod muscle.

Next we'll be working with the clod muscle.

1. Start by trimming any exterior fat and silver skin from the main muscle.

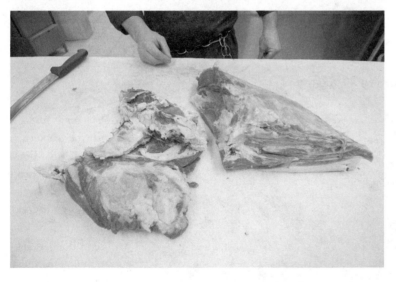

2. Once you have the trim removed from the clod, it's time to clean up the main muscle for use as a roast. These tough muscles require some slow braising and are ready to be wrapped as soon as the fat is trimmed.

3. Using your boning knife, slide it under the tough silver skin and remove any unwanted, chewy bits.

BUTCHER'S TIP

The clod muscle is a tough one because of its location, and therefore it requires some slow braising to gain its full effect and tenderness. Consider tying this roast to create a uniform shape ideal for cooking evenly.

Remove the brisket.

The brisket is the next piece to be removed.

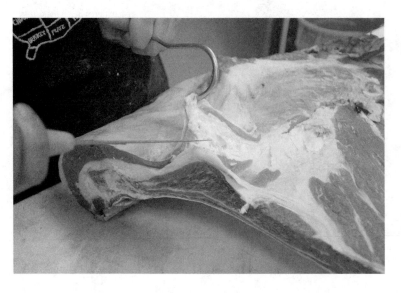

1. There's a seam just beneath the brisket muscle that will allow you to remove it with ease, it's just a matter of locating it. Go too deep and you'll be into the breast bone; don't go deep enough, and you'll be cutting into the brisket itself. Go slowly and monitor your progress.

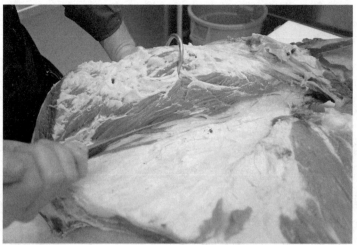

2. Once the correct seam has been located, use your breaking hook, to apply pressure by pulling with your hook and releasing the muscle with your knife.

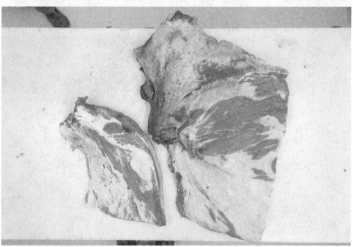

3. Cut following the breast plate. This is where the term double brisket, or brisket point, came about. Considered to be the most prized part of the brisket, the double end contains the most amount of fat and is great for smoking or braising.

4. Remove and discard any heavy fat. This is a perfect slow cooking cut, so it's good to leave a decent amount of fat for self-basting.

Remove the chain muscle.

What's left now are two major usable cuts: the blade and the chuck short ribs. We've saved the best for last, as both require some decent knife skills in order to obtain the desired cuts without leaving too much meat on the bones.

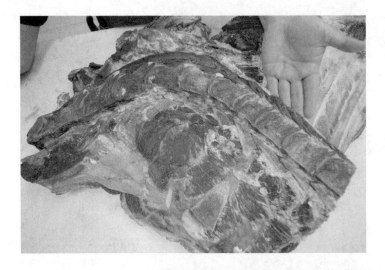

1. Locate what's known as the *chain*. It's a small muscle that runs the length of the spine from the head to the shoulder.

2. Use the tip of your knife to run along the length of the spine. Think savvy on this cut. Work carefully along the curves of the vertebrae, staying as close to the bones as possible. After the chain muscle has been removed, add it to the grind bucket for later use.

WARNING

Using your knife becomes increasingly difficult as you move toward the head. Grooves and crevices are tricky to get around, but with each movement of your knife you'll become more familiar with how the skeletal features affect your efforts. There are lots of ins and outs when working along the spine, so this is a good time to brush up on your knife skills!

Remove the neck bones.

Removing the neck bones can be the trickiest cuts you'll have to make on the entire carcass.

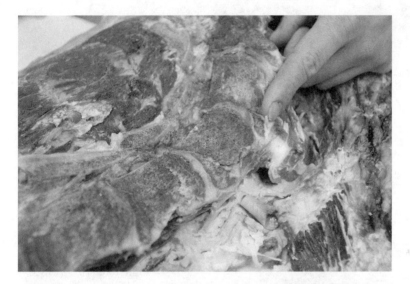

1. Locate the vertebrae closest to the neck just after the first rib on the chuck. Use the top one third of your boning knife for maximum flexibility when cutting.

2. Make an incision through the vertebrae to loosen up the joint. This will be your starting point for removing the neck bones. Your knife should easily go through the spine joint just above the first rib.

3. Cut carefully along the bones of the neck to cut the meat loose. Apply pressure by pulling on the bones as you release them with your knife.

WARNING

This is where patience plays an important role in your attempts at butchery. With your boning knife, you'll be moving in and out of nooks and crevices all along the neck bones. This is where the utmost caution is to be used, as your hands will be extremely close to the blade.

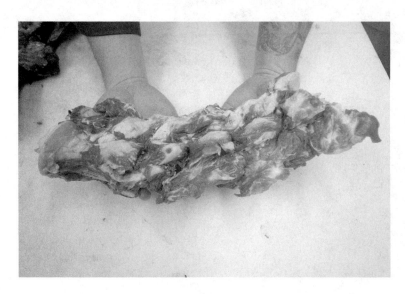

4. The end result is a run of neck bones ready to be used as one of the most flavor-filled additions to a stew or stock pot. Clean any meat remaining to be used for grounds later on.

Separate the blade muscle from the short ribs.

Next we separate the blade muscle from the short ribs.

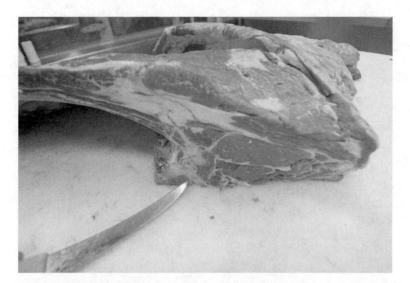

1. Locate the gap where the spinal cord runs nearest to the location where you separated the rib from the chuck. A small groove in the bones is an easy marker.

2. Run your knife up to where the main blade muscle begins and make another mark.

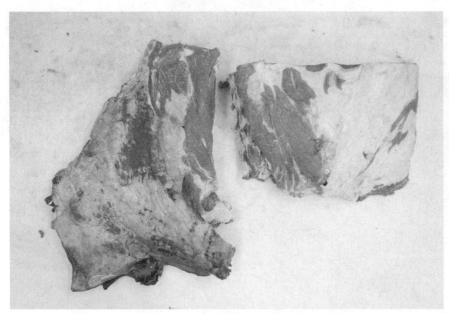

3. The blade has now been separated from the short ribs, and both will need additional cleaning.

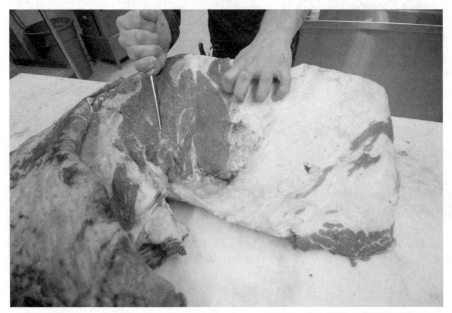

4. Much like the rib before, the blade also has a back strap running the length of the muscle. We'll need to peel back some meat to expose and remove it.

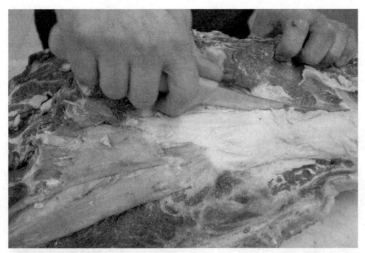

5. Make a mark between the spots you've marked off and then follow through with a deeper cut, down to the feather bones beneath.

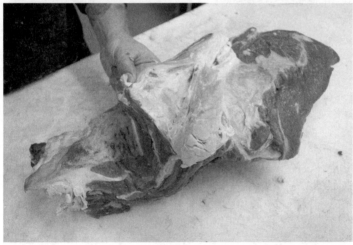

6. Similar to the pork shoulder, you'll now need to remove any heavy fat—paying close attention to remove the ever present gland that is located in the heavy fat of the lower neck.

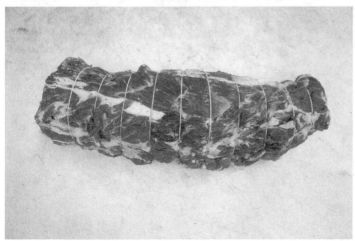

7. Once the blade has been cleaned up to your liking, there are a few things you can do: tie it up as a roast, cut it into ranch steaks, cut it up for stew, or grind it into the most amazing ground beef.

Remove the chuck short ribs.

The chuck short ribs are an absolute favorite. Slowly braising for hours in a flavorful braising liquid yields some of the most flavorful and filling meals. It's a challenge to finish one on your own, let alone trying to tackle them all! Invite some friends over, have a beverage, and enjoy some good aromas in the air while you wait.

1. Remove the chine bones from the short ribs. Using your free hand to secure the ribs, cut through with a bone saw.

2. Mark off where you'll be separating your ribs from the breast bone. Take care to not short change yourself on the amount of meat you'll want on the ribs and the amount that'll stay on the breast bone.

3. Cut where the meat tapers down to preserve a good amount of meat on both sides.

Clean up the ribs.

Once you've separated the breast bone and the ribs, it's now time to clean up the ribs.

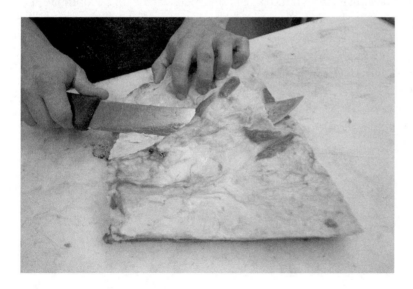

1. Clean any usable meat from the breast bone for use in grinding later. Remove any exterior fat and silver skin.

2. Cut between each of the four ribs to get your nice meaty short ribs ready for the slow cooker.

As you can see, the process of breaking down all the large beef sections can be time consuming and involved; however, you will end up with enough meat to fill a large freezer. Last time we butchered a year-old steer his hanging weight (called gross weight) was 600 pounds, and we split more than 400 pounds of finished cuts and ground meat with my in-laws. A full cow will feed an average size family for a year, so it's definitely an investment that can be worthwhile to you, especially when sourcing grass-fed or organic-raised beef. When you do the majority of the butchering yourself as shown in these pages, you'll realize not only an increased savings, but also the satisfaction that comes from making yourself part of the process.

Lamb, Venison, and Goat 4

Lamb is a popular meat choice for many home butchers because these animals can be raised in a small space, have an easy-to-handle size, and have flavorful meat. Even a full-grown sheep has well-marbled meat that, while leaner than beef, is not too tough. It is, however, one of those love-it-or-hate-it types of meat.

While lamb is considered a red meat, they are more easily found as grass- or pasture-finished animals, increasing the amount of heart-healthy omega-3 fatty acids. Lamb meat is high in usable iron, many trace minerals, and of course, an excellent source of protein.

Similar in anatomy to lamb, deer and goats are one of the most popular meat animals worldwide. They thrive in a variety of terrains and only require a low level of feed to produce delicious, lean meat. The steps shown here show photos of a lamb, so we use the term "lamb" throughout the chapter; however, they are applicable to deer and goats as well.

Introducing the Animal

Lamb will be broken into several useful and delicious cuts, including meat for sausage, chops, tenderloin, shanks (great for braising), slow cooking roasts, and more. Sheep have 13 pairs of ribs (so do cows) and are usually processed as a whole, not split like cattle. This is because of their smaller size—the average lamb is between 45 and 60 pounds. In fact, if you are a hunter familiar with working up your own deer, you will find lamb an easy animal to manage since the size and confirmation is so similar.

We will be breaking down the lamb entirely from whole carcass to individual cuts. In the next section, you will see how to break down the animal into individual sections. Then you will learn how to work each section up into the specific cuts.

For example, you'll first learn how to cut the lamb into six workable parts, such as saddle, shoulders, etc. Then you'll learn how to take each part into smaller cuts, so the shoulders, for example, will become bone-in roasts and several chops.

The Main Breakdown

The primal cuts are the main sections, in this case shoulders, neck, *loin* (the back), ribs, saddle, legs, and shanks. When working with a whole lamb carcass, it is easy to break down the main pieces and then work up each one from there. This makes it easier to maneuver each part and allows you to keep the rest of the meat safely cooled.

a. leg   c. loin   e. shoulder   g. breast   i. fore shank

b. sirloin   d. rack   f. neck   h. hind shank

Remove the Front Shoulders

First we will start by separating the front shoulders. You'll find that lamb shoulder is naturally flavorful and turns into great roasts or sometimes chops.

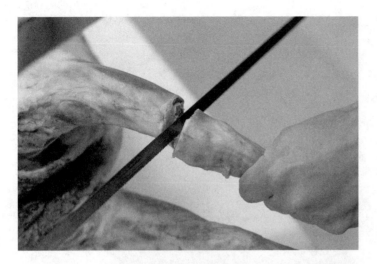

1. Remove the lower legs below the knee joint. Bend the knee slightly to help you find and expose the joint. This joint has tough ligaments and tendons, so you'll want to use a bone saw instead of a knife. Remove on both the left and right sides. The lower leg bones are generally discarded.

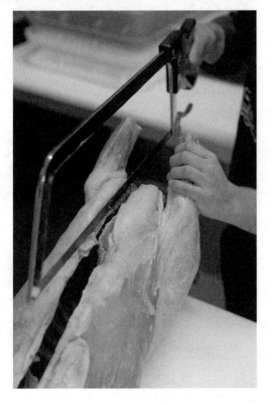

2. If your carcass hasn't been split in the chest cavity you'll want to do that now. Use a bone saw to cut through the breast bone and expose the inside of the rib cage. Some lamb carcasses will come with the chest cavity already opened, but sometimes a home butcher will need to do that himself or herself.

3. Once the chest is split, pull the sides apart, exposing the ribs. Count from the neck area down until you've found the third rib.

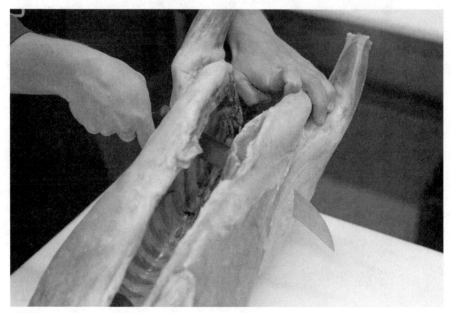

4. Use your long knife to make a cut between the third and fourth ribs. You'll be pushing the knife (blade side up) through both sides.

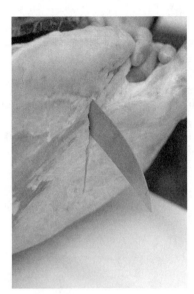

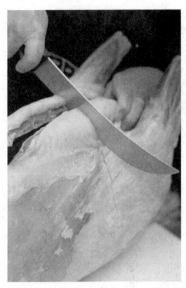

5. Make a cut upward through the rib cage about 7 or 8 inches long. You'll feel resistance when you reach the bones.

6. Pull your long knife out carefully and turn it blade down. You'll use the blade to score the meat so you have a cut line to follow with your bone saw.

7. Now switch to your bone saw and saw through the bones downward until you reach your earlier knife cut.

8. Once you've met your earlier cut, begin to pull apart the shoulders from the spine to give yourself room for your saw blade.

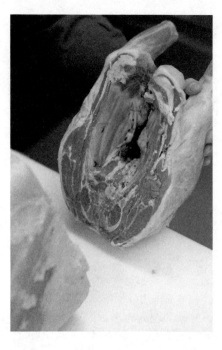

9. Cut through the shoulder rack and spine until you've completely separated the shoulders, neck, and front shanks section from the body of the lamb.

Place the meat in the fridge until you're ready to work it up further, as we will show in the section "Foreshanks and Brisket" of this chapter.

Remove the Belly and Back Legs

Now we will move on to removing the ribs and belly meat before removing the back legs.

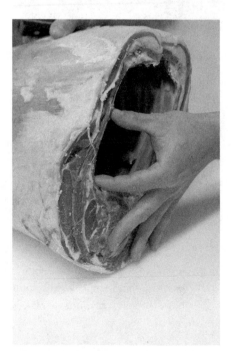

1. Measure about 5 inches up from the spine in the rack eye. The rack eye is the opening at the front of the lamb after you've removed the front shoulder section.

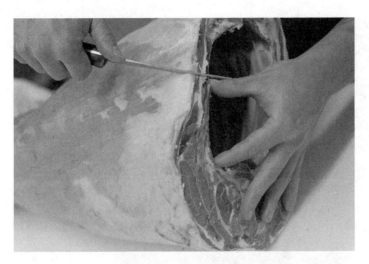

2. Use your long knife to score the flesh on the outside of the ribs until you reach the belly section. This will be your cut line to remove the rib tips and belly meat from the lamb.

3. Now switch to the bone saw and cut along your mark. Use your free hand to lift the meat and separate it. Here the butcher is cutting with his right hand and grasping the belly meat with his left hand.

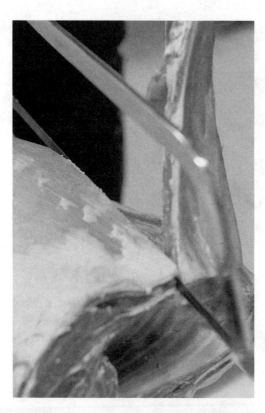

4. Continue cutting through the bones with the hand saw as you pull the belly away from the ribs until you've freed the belly from the carcass completely.

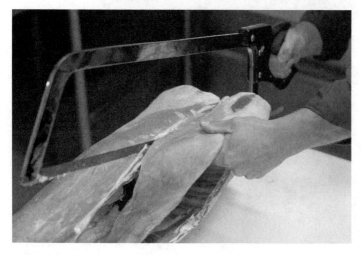

5. Roll the lamb over and repeat these steps on the second side.

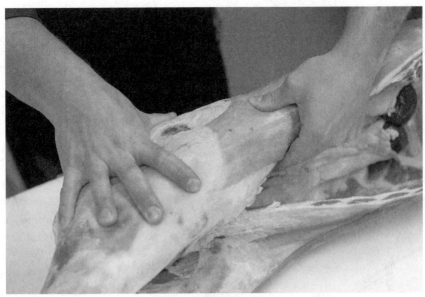

6. To remove the back legs from the lamb, you'll want to cut the meat where the back legs attach to the spine. Find the thinnest part of the waist and feel for the hip bone with your hand.

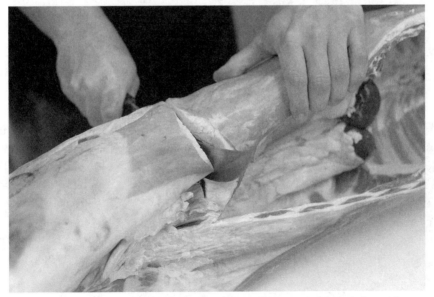

7. Cut with your long knife all the way through the muscle (just above the point of the hip) until you reach the spine. You will be cutting through the *white bone,* or cartilage, which is tough but soft enough to cut with your knife.

DEFINITION

Meat, cartilage, and other soft tissues are cut with a knife. Bones are cut with a saw. Cartilage is often called **white bone** by butchers and is cut with knives.

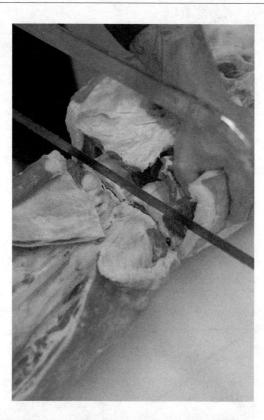

8. Once you've released the muscle on both sides, use the bone saw to cut through the spine, completely detaching the back legs and hips from the body of the lamb. When cutting the loin free, make your cuts as close to the hip bones as you can in order to preserve as much of the valuable loin meat as possible.

9. Now you'll have the loins and ribs of the lamb, often called the saddle. The saddle of the lamb (to the left) and the recently removed back legs with sirloin, rib eye, and other cuts (to the right) are shown here.

Break Down the Saddle

The saddle contains both the loins and the ribs. Your carcass may also have the kidneys still attached, so we will remove those and separate the rack of lamb (rib area) from the loins.

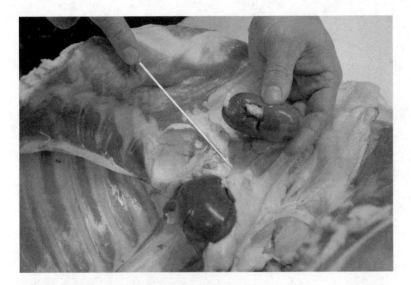

1. To remove the kidneys, simply hold one kidney in your hand and lift it up away from the back of the lamb. Use a small knife to cut the connective tissue holding the kidney in place. Repeat to remove the other kidney.

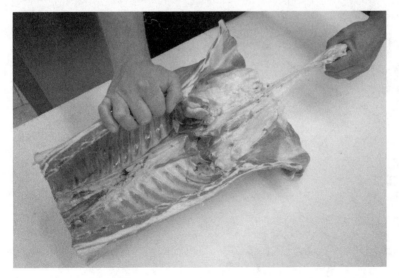

2. There may be gristle, fat, or even pieces of the liver in this area once the kidneys are removed. Some of it can be taken out by hand. Just grasp the loose fat and pull it out.

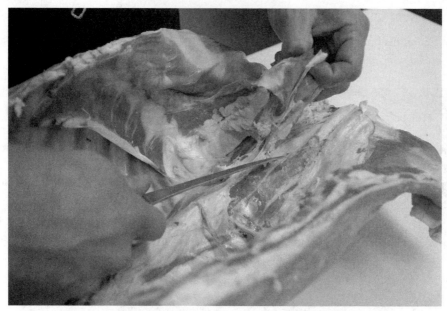

3. Trim up the rest by cutting it out with a small butcher knife, taking care not to puncture the tenderloin with your knife.

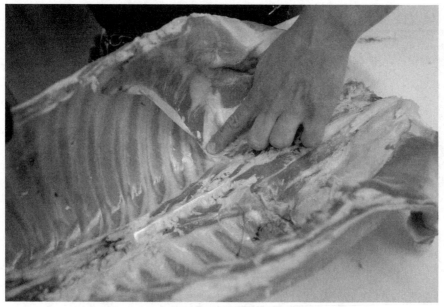

4. Use your finger to find the last full rib on the rack. It will be the last long bone stretching all the way from the spine.

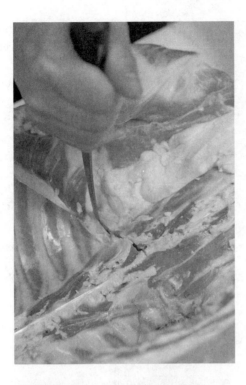

5. Insert your knife blade from just above the vertebra of the spine below the last rib. Remember to try to keep your cuts as even as possible so the loin section will be almost square.

6. Cut through the meat to separate the rib rack from the loins with one, smooth upward motion.

WARNING

When separating the rib rack from the loins, be sure you are standing to one side as you lift your blade upward to make the cut. The knives are sharp enough to cut flesh, and that includes yours if you get in the way!

7. Repeat this cut on the other side of the torso so you've cut through the meat on both sides.

8. The saddle should lay open and be ready for you to clean up the cut and remove completely.

9. Bring the rack to the edge of the counter or worktable and bend it open to completely separate the loin from the rack. Use your knife to make the cut as clean as possible to avoid tearing the meat when we finish the cut later. Cut through any remaining meat until you've reached all the way to the bone of the vertebrae.

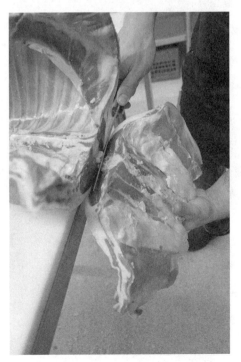

10. Bend the joint back over the counter even further, exposing the space between the vertebra, and use your knife to finish the cut. You won't be cutting with the bone saw because you are just going to slip your knife between the bones; you are not cutting through the bones.

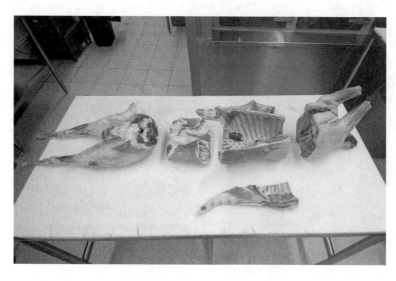

11. Now your lamb is broken down into main sections.

In the next section, we'll walk you through the process of creating those beautiful, usable cuts of meat that you'll find mentioned in recipes.

Making the Cuts

This section includes the many cuts you will recognize from common recipes and grocery store aisles. You'll now be creating the individual or main *retail* cuts.

Foreshanks and Brisket

The foreshanks are like shin bones on a sheep. Foreshanks are often used in a braised dish. The meat at the end of the foreshanks will include the brisket meat from the chest area. The brisket is removed and later ground for mince lamb.

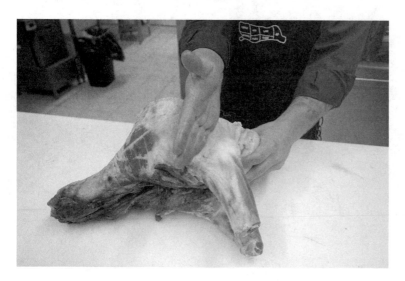

1. Make your cut so it is parallel to the line of the shoulders—where the hand in the photo is square to the back of the shoulders.

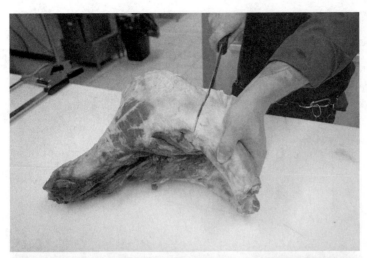

2. Use your long knife to cut your mark through the meat down to the bones.

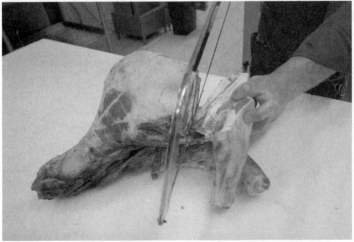

3. Use your bone saw to cut through the bones of the foreleg until you've separated it from the shoulders.

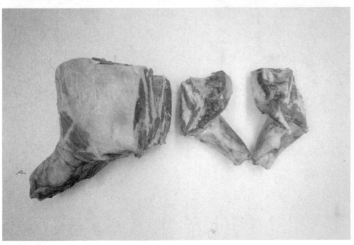

4. Cut through the second leg as well (you should be able to do it all in one cut without flipping over the lamb) until the two foreshanks are removed.

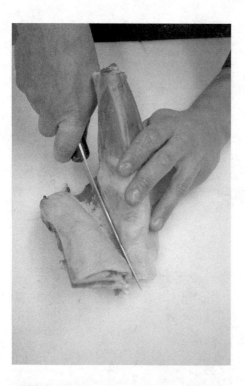

5. Some of the meat at the end of the foreshanks will include the brisket meat from the chest area. Cut this extra meat off with your butcher's knife. The foreshanks are now ready to be wrapped and frozen or cooked fresh. The brisket meat you removed, however, will need to be trimmed before it is ready.

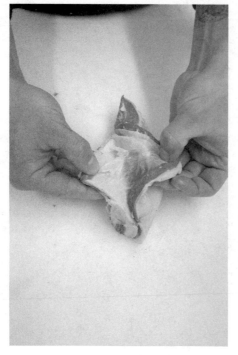

6. There is a thick layer of fat that needs to be removed from the tender brisket meat. You should be able to simply peel the fat from the meat.

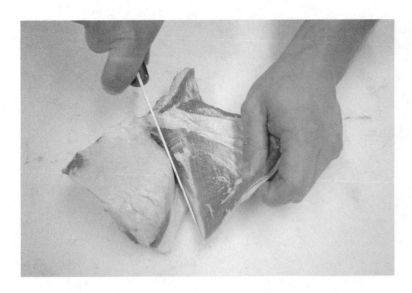

7. Continue to peel the fat away, carefully using a short knife when needed to cut the fascia layers connecting the fat to the meat.

Once you've trimmed and discarded the fat from the brisket, you'll be ready to package the meat and put it in the fridge or freezer.

The Neck

You will now be removing the neck from the shoulders, working as closely to the shoulder section as possible.

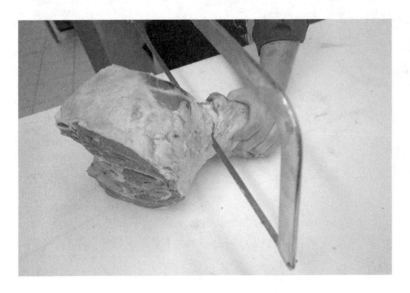

1. Firmly grasp the neck lay your saw blade on the neck right against the shoulders. Cut firmly through the neck with the hand saw until you are completely through the bone.

2. Once you're through the bone, switch to the knife to get through the meat quickly.

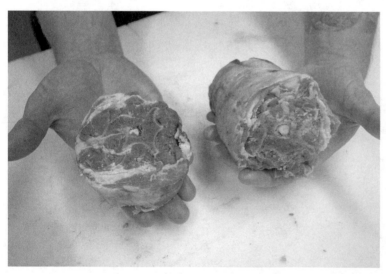

3. Cut through the neck bones to section it into two or three individual pieces. These can be easily used in ragùs or stews.

The shoulder section will become bone-in roasts and other goodies, but first you have to split them. We will show how to prepare a simple bone-in roast with the first shoulder and how to cut chops with the second shoulder.

The Shoulders

The shoulders of lamb are best cooked slowly over low heat to preserve the tenderness. Chops can be cooked roasted, broiled, panfried, or even grilled. This section is going to show you how to prepare a roast with the first shoulder and chops with the second shoulder.

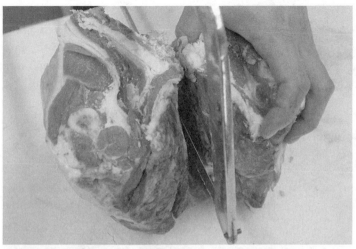

1. Cut through the middle of the shoulder section with the bone saw until you're completely through the boney area and the two sides fall open.

2. From here you can use your knife to cut through the remaining meat pieces to fully separate the two shoulder pieces.

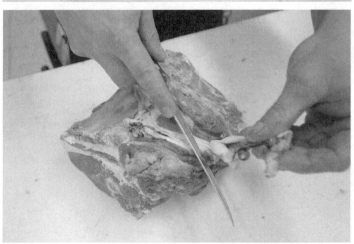

3. With the first shoulder, trim away any excess fat or bloody bits on the inside of the shoulder or, as in this case, an area where there was a vein in the fat leading up to the neck.

4. Flip the shoulder over so the back is up (the inside down on the table) and tie the roast. Simply loop the butcher's twine around the roast and tie it tightly.

BUTCHER'S TIP

Tying the roast will allow the meat to stay in a nice tight package during the cooking process, which in this case will be a delicious slow-roast. Refer to Appendix C for more information.

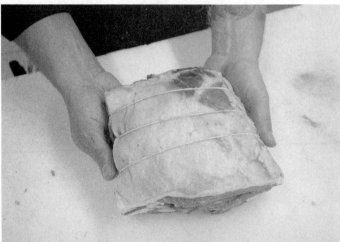

5. Use common sense when judging the width of your individual shoulder to determine if it needs three or four ties. This roast took three lengths of string to tie well.

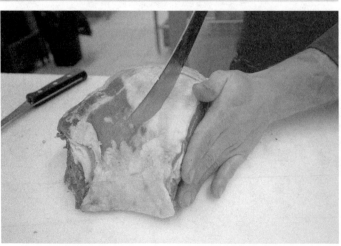

6. With the second shoulder, you will start from the loin side of the shoulder. Measure a good width for your chops. This first cut is about 1¼ inches. Cut through the meat with your long knife until you reach the bone of the shoulder.

7. Switch to your bone saw to finish the cut.

8. Each chop is now ready to be wrapped and frozen or placed in the fridge for fresh eating. Continue to cut the shoulder into chops at even intervals until you've completed working up this shoulder.

Leg of Lamb

Now we'll work the backshanks and flank areas to create delicious leg of lamb and sirloin cuts. We will show the first leg as a simple bone-in leg-of-lamb, which is the fastest way to butcher it. With the second leg, you'll be able to see the steps for removing the bones from the leg. The process takes a little more time, but it will yield a fabulous roast as well as tender sirloin cuts.

Prepare a bone-in leg roast.

We will be using the first lamb leg to prepare this roast. You can always use this procedure on both legs if you prefer bone-in leg roast. Cook it on a low heat for maximum tenderness.

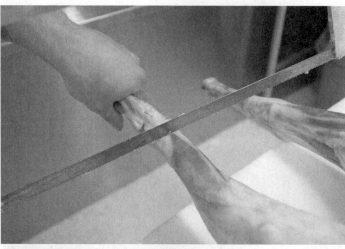

1. Take off the lower leg at the joint by using a bone saw to cut through the leg bone. Repeat with the other leg; discard the lower bone segments.

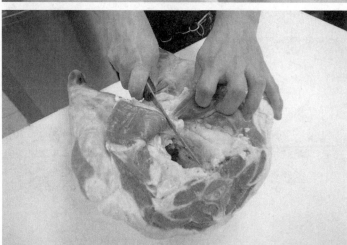

2. Now cut the two sides in half. Use a boning knife to cut through the meat until you reach bone. Make sure the valuable sirloin meat is held out of the way when cutting the haunches.

3. Switch to a bone saw to finish the cut once you can't go any further with your knife. Saw through the bones until you've split the legs apart.

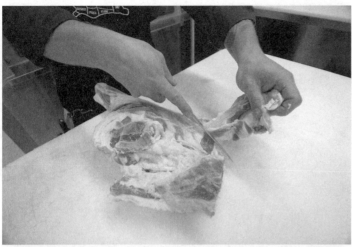

4. There's usually a thicker layer of fat on the back edge of the shank (the sirloin area) that can be trimmed off with the boning knife.

5. Set your knife tip as shown in the photo. There is a seam in the meat where it should be relatively easy to insert your knife into. Peel and cut open the meat along this seam to expose the tailbone. Removing the tailbone can be tricky, as it takes some force and knife wiggling to get it out.

6. Cut through to get behind the tailbone and cut it completely free from the leg, preserving as much of the meat as possible.

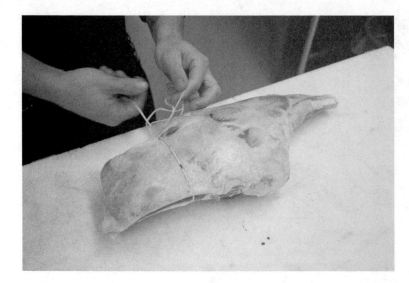

7. Fold the meat back over where the tailbone was and tie it closed for a bone-in roast. We are finished with the first lamb leg.

Prepare a bone-in sirloin roast.

We will begin preparing this sirloin roast using the second leg of lamb. Again, if you prefer bone-in sirloin roast and butterflied leg of lamb, you can always use these procedures on both legs. A bone-in sirloin roast is a nice option for feeding smaller numbers—two or three adults can eat well from one roast.

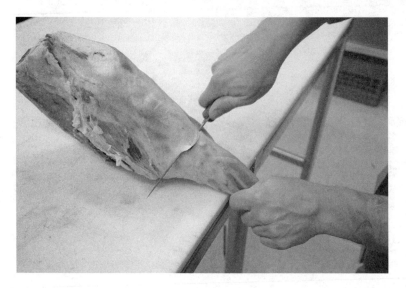

1. Feel for the top of the shank bone until the feel the bump of the knee. That's where you want to make your cut to remove the shank bone.

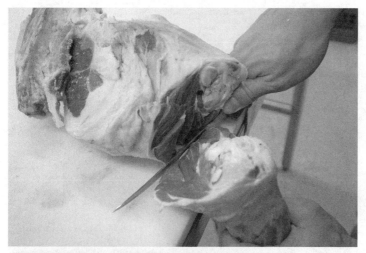

2. Bend the joint open in order to slip your knife through the joint. (Use the correct force as you bend it to open it slightly.) Cut the rear shank off completely using the knife to cut both ligaments and meat. Keep the shank for slow braising.

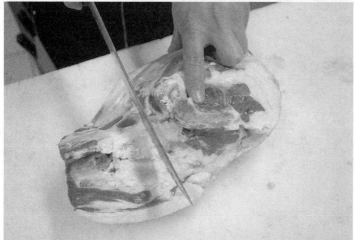

3. Mark the meat about an inch above the aitchbone to separate the sirloin portion from the leg. Make your knife cut mark on both edges so you can flip it over and still see your marks to match them.

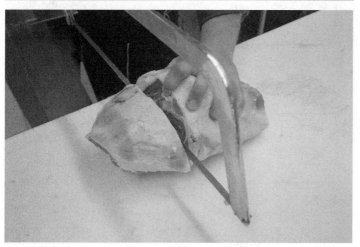

4. Cut through the meat with your knife to remove the sirloin roast, using the bone saw as needed to finish the cut.

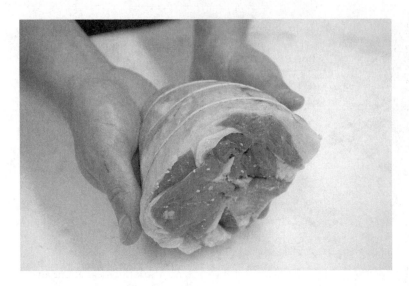

5. Tie the sirloin roast as needed to pack it tight for cooking as a bone-in sirloin roast.

Prepare a butterflied leg of lamb.

We separated the leg from the sirloin in step 3 of the previous section, "Prepare a bone-in sirloin roast." This leg portion is where we now turn our attention. We will remove the aitch and femur bones to completely debone the leg.

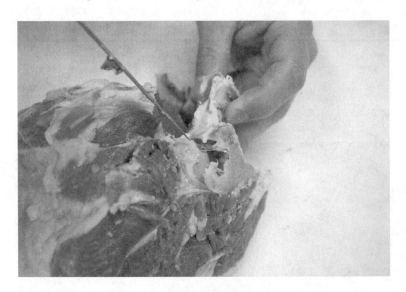

1. Use the tip of your knife to cut around the round top of the aitchbone to try to avoid cutting the meat as much as possible. Sever the connective tissues that hold the meat to the bone all the way around the bone and remove the aitchbone.

BUTCHER'S TIP

The aitchbone is hard to remove because it is a rounded bone on top. Don't be afraid to use a variety of angles to loosen the meat from around the bone, and use only the first inch to inch and a half of the knife tip.

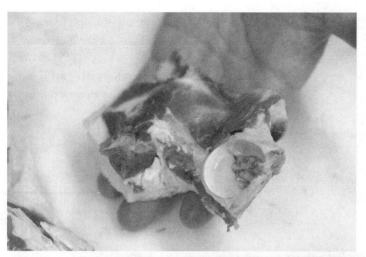

2. The off shape of the aitchbone can be difficult to work; the trick is to keep the knife as close as possible to the bone.

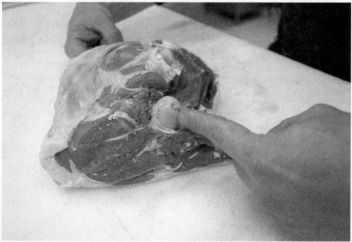

3. Now we are going to remove the second bone, the femur. Find the points of the leg bone with your fingers so you can clearly see how the bone is positioned.

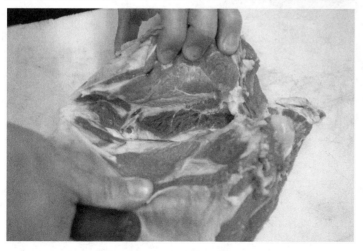

4. Make a smooth cut along the line of the bone, cutting through the meat on the top of the leg until you reach the bone. Pay attention to the direction of the bone and work closely to the bone so you don't cut into the meat too much. Pull the meat apart to expose the bone.

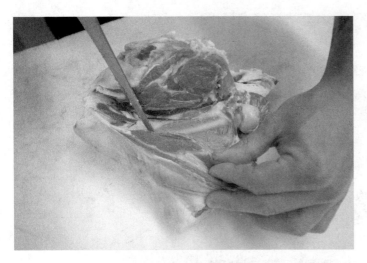

5. Now use the tip of your knife to cut the meat away from both sides of the bone. Remember your goal is to cut as close to the bone as possible.

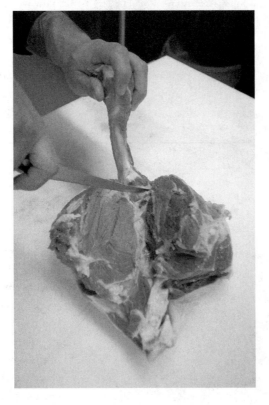

6. Continue cutting until you are able to remove the bone completely.

7. Now that you've removed the bone, you should see how the meat of the leg has begun to open up. There is a natural seam in the meat that you can use to butterfly the leg of lamb. Pull back the inside round steak and use the knife as needed to open it along the seam without completely cutting through.

8. Find the vein in the inside of the round steak so you can remove it. The opening of the vein is visible at the tip of the knife in the photo.

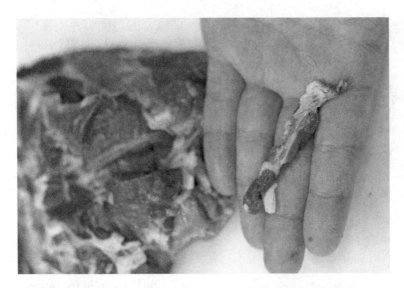

9. Make a few careful incisions to enable you to remove the vein without having to cut completely through the steak.

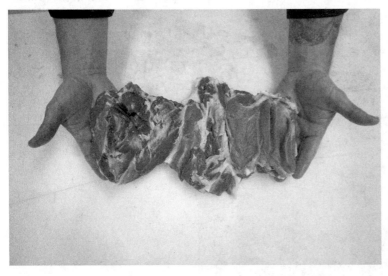

10. Your butterflied leg of lamb will provide delicious steaks for your family. You can also bake or broil it in half the time now that it's butterflied open instead of a thicker, harder-to-cook, whole portion.

Loins

The loin meat is juicy and tender when cooked. This makes it a prized cut. The steps in this section will help you prepare delicious roasts and other cuts.

Prepare a bone-in loin roast.

The loin roast is considered one of the best cuts on the lamb. When you break the cuts up you can sauté them for tender meat strips, or you can save them as full roasts. Loin roasts are perfect for a family meal.

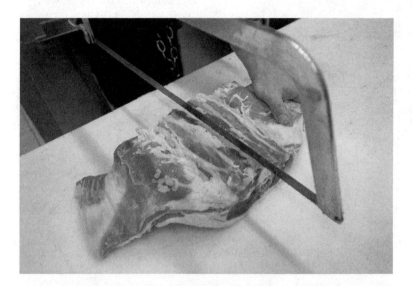

1. Use the bone saw to cut the loins exactly in half. There is a defined, natural line you can follow to make your cut.

2. Remove the spinal cord from the spinal column by scrapping it out with your knife.

3. Now remove the excess fat that sits below the tenderloin. There's a natural seam that allows you to scrape the fat off. Remove the excess fat from the top as well, to clean up the loins before rolling.

4. Fold the loins over themselves so the meat wraps around the column of the spine.

5. Trim the excess uneven "tail meat" that overhangs the roll.

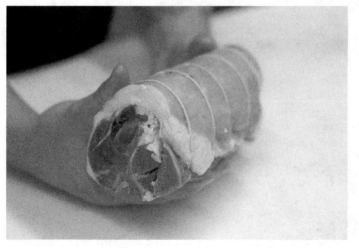

6. Tie the roll of meat tight and even with butcher's twine and cook as a bone-in roast. The tender meat of the loin makes it a favorite.

Prepare loin chops.

We will show the second loin cut into chops. The procedure is similar to the previous section, "Prepare a bone-in loin roast." Start by cleaning any spinal cord from the spinal column and removing the fat that sits below the tenderloin (steps 2 and 3 in the previous section).

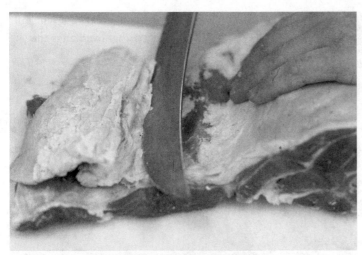

1. Trim away all the excess fat and heavy fat until you've reached the meat. Just peel the fat off the top side of the meat.

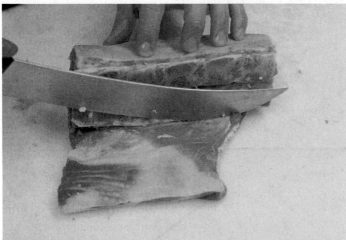

2. Roll it over so you can trim the thin side of the uneven tail meat to make it square.

BUTCHER'S TIP

The trimmed "tail meat" can be saved for stew meat, added to chili, or ground. It is usable meat, so don't toss it!

3. Now unfold the loin and roll it tightly, beginning with the thin side of the meat. Note this technique is different than rolling the roast in the previous section (where the meat is wrapped around the column of the spine).

4. Square the roll up by cutting the edges even with the bone of the spine. You may need to use the bone saw to do this and then clean it up with the knife.

5. Mark even cuts to create your chops based on the length of your loin section. In this case, four thick chops is a good number.

6. Cut through the sections with your knife until you reach bone and then finish the cuts with a bone saw. The finished chops look beautiful and are ready to cook.

Ribs

The last section left to be worked up is the rack of ribs. We will be splitting the ribs in half, cutting them as a whole rack and then frenching the rack of ribs.

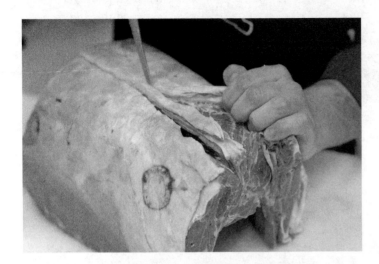

1. Place the ribs with the back side up. Make two hard cuts on each side of the spine as deep as you can with your knife.

2. Now turn the rib rack over and cut through the spine with the bone saw. This will divide the ribs into two separate racks.

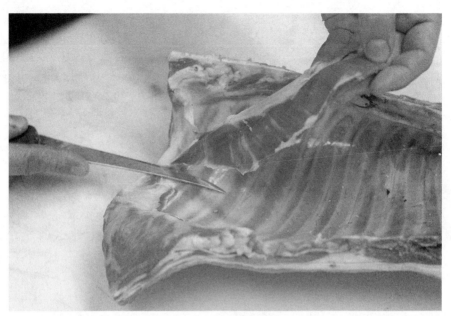

3. Remove the extra meat (called the skirt steak) from the rib rack and set it aside to go in the fridge or freezer.

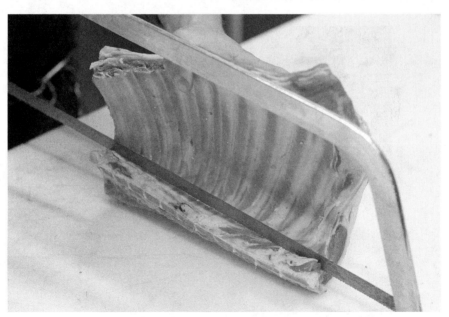

4. Now cut the spine off the end of the ribs with the bone saw.

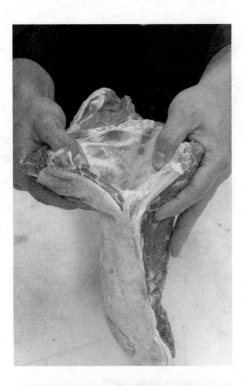

5. The ribs are covered in a thick layer of fatty meat on the top side called a cap. You will need to remove the cap and can use it for grinding.

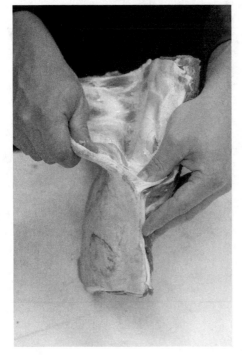

6. Insert your fingers into the natural seam and pull the cap from the ribs.

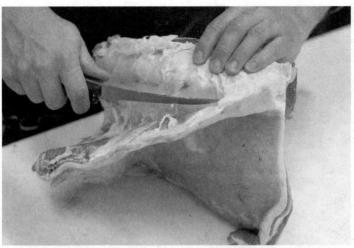

7. Use your knife as needed to cut the connective fascia so you can fully remove the fatty layer. Don't score the rib meat, just follow the natural line between ribs and cap.

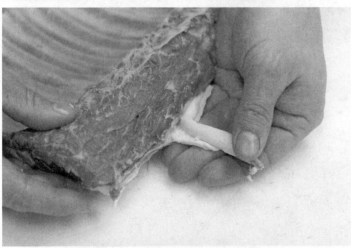

8. Remove the backstrap from the spine side of the ribs. This thick back of fat and connective tissue should come out completely.

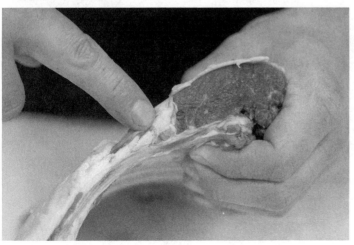

9. Now that you've separated the rib rack from the rest of the lamb you will be ready to french the ribs. This treatment allows more even results during the cooking process. Find the eye of the ribs, located just above the thick rack meat.

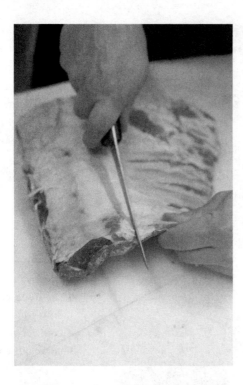

10. You'll make your incision about ¼ of an inch on the bone side of the eye. Score the ribs just above the eye at each end of the rib rack.

11. Make a strong cut all the way down the ribs, matching the marks you made on each end.

12. Now use your knife to remove the meat from the top of the rib bones, starting at the cut you made on one end and pulling toward the other end of the ribs.

13. Cut through the cartilage tips of the ribs to even the cut and make the frenching look better.

14. Mark between each rib by pulling your knife along the big cut from step 11, letting the tip sink through the meat between each bone.

15. Flip the ribs over and do the same thing, going the opposite direction. Be sure you stay even with the cuts you just made so you are reinforcing those cuts.

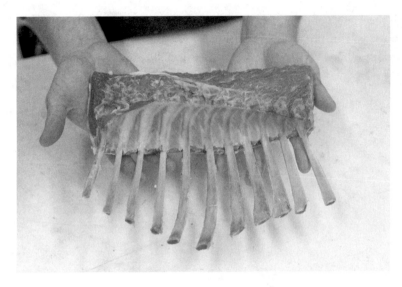

16. Stand the ribs up and work your knife in between each rib, removing the meat to the point of the cut you made.

BUTCHER'S TIP

Did you know that frenching the ribs has not only a cosmetic but also a practical purpose? The thinner meat of the ribs will cook much faster than the thicker meat of the rack. So by removing the meat from between the ribs, it is easier to cook the rack of ribs to an even, delicious perfection.

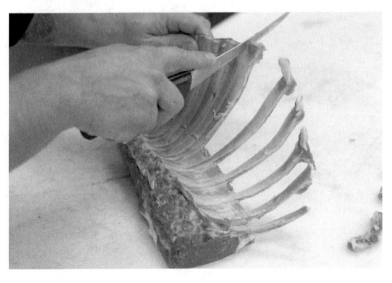

17. Make sure you cut close to the bone on both sides of each rib to remove all the meat in between. Scraping the bits of meat off the bone will help prevent charring when you cook the rack of ribs. The final result is a finished, polished look that will have your friends and family amazed at your butchering skills!

You don't have to go through the trouble of doing this type of cut for home eating, but it makes a nice change of pace. Just because you are doing your own home cuts doesn't mean you can't explore gourmet options. In fact, cutting your own meat gives you greater flexibility with your cuts and budget considerations.

Pork ∞ 5

Pork is an animal that produces more meat than many people realize. Most pigs are butchered at a few months old, when the carcass size will be easy to work up. Pork is flavorful and tender, making it a favorite meat choice in the United States.

Introducing the Animal

Pork is a favored meat for the homesteader or home butcher because it produces one of the highest percentages of usable meat for carcass weight, compared to other meat animals. It is a favorite meat for many foodies and provides good sized cuts for the average family use. An average small-size carcass will produce 150 to 200 pounds of meat after processing, making it a quick way to fill the freezer. The main primal sections are the shoulder, rib rack, belly, loin, and leg of pork.

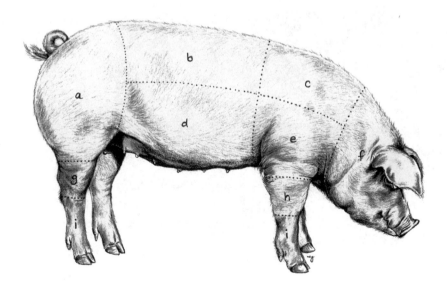

a. leg   c. boston butt   e. picnic shoulder   g. hind hock   i. trotters

b. loin   d. belly   f. head   h. fore hock

The Main Breakdown

This animal has been skinned at the abbatoir before being sold as a whole carcass to the butcher shop. Sometimes they will be available and still have the skin and hair on them, so for easier home processing, check with your local source before purchasing to get your animal without skin. If you have a skinless animal, the need for plunging in hot water or scraping the hide is eliminated.

1. Beginning with a full side of pork, we will be breaking this half of the pig into the main primal sections, which will be easier to work up into individual cuts.

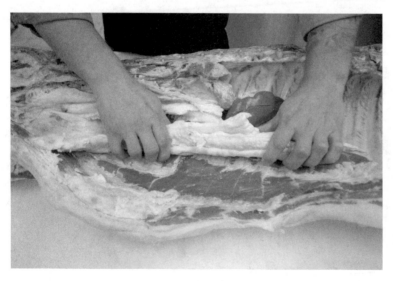

2. Find the leaf lard inside the body cavity of the pig. This line of fat inside the body cavity is the best quality fat on the pig. It is often what's used for rendering into lard.

3. Pull the leaf fat back and up to separate it from the ribs and belly to remove it completely.

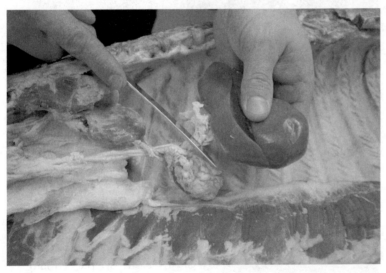

4. If it is still present, cut through the vein holding the kidney in place to remove it from the body cavity. Kidneys can be cooked when properly prepared.

Now we will begin breaking down the side of pork. The pork side is easier to work up than a beef carcass because of the more manageable size. We'll start by removing the shoulder and proceed to working up the individual cuts.

Remove the Shoulder

Now we will be removing the front shoulders from the rib rack.

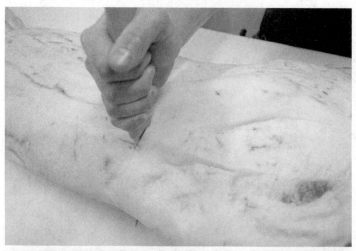

1. Count three ribs in from the head down and make your knife marks between the third and fourth rib. Pierce through the meat between the ribs to mark the cut line for separating the front shoulder.

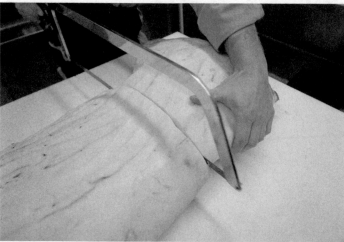

2. Use the bone saw to cut along your marks. Cut through the blade bone and top of the rib cage to remove the front shoulder from the rib rack.

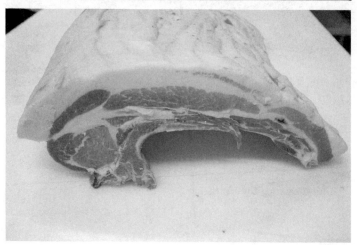

3. Once the shoulder has been removed, you can clearly see the marbling throughout that will give the meat excellent flavor.

Remove the Leg and Rib Rack

Now that the shoulder is removed, we can move on to the leg and remove the leg from the sirloin. The goal is to preserve the tender sirloin meat as you remove the leg.

1. Begin your cut about 2 inches above the aitchbone, using the knife to cut deeply through the flesh that attaches the belly to the leg. Continue cutting until you reach bone.

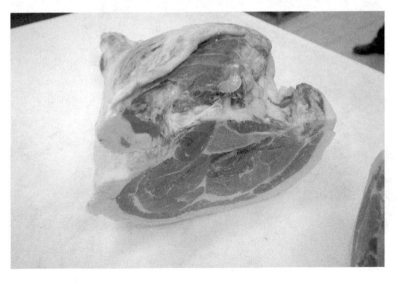

2. Cut to remove the leg from the sirloin. Then use the bone saw to finish the cut so you've completely removed the leg section. The leg can now to be set aside to work up later.

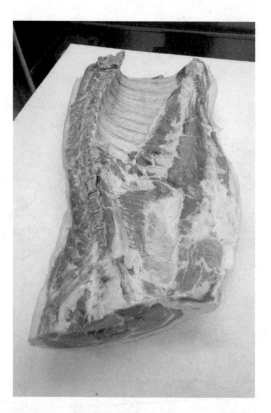

3. This is what the side of pork looks like after the front shoulder and leg have been removed. We will be removing the belly meat from the ribs to make this section ready for a variety of cuts.

4. To remove the eye of the rib, you'll want to measure two fingers from the eye of the ribs.

5. Score the meat with your knife and then make a second pass to cut through all the meat between each of the ribs. Use the bone saw to cut through the ribs and remove the eye of the ribs.

6. The rack of ribs is ready to be further processed into the various cuts of pork now that the eye of the ribs has been cut away.

The Cuts of Pork

A pig is a very flexible animal in terms of how you process the primals and turn them into final cuts. For example, the rib rack can be cleaned up and cooked as a rack of ribs, or as we will show, it can be processed as individual chops.

A CUT ABOVE

As with much of the information presented in these chapters, feel free to experiment as you gain confidence in your abilities, to develop your own style and preferred methods. Let the suggestions be a starting point for your home butchering journey.

Rack and Belly

Now that you have your side of pork ready to be worked up, we will remove the side ribs from the tender belly meat. You have some choices here about how much meat you want to leave on the belly.

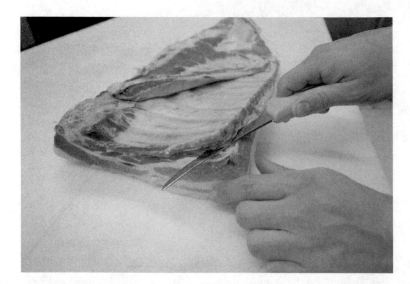

1. Use your knife to cut through the edge of the meat to mark your desired thickness.

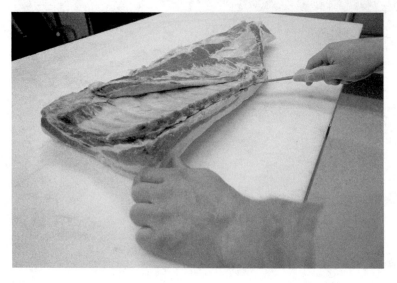

2. Score the meat all along the rib line to make the initial cut for thickness so it's easier to separate the ribs from the belly.

3. Pull the ribs up and away from the belly, using the knife as needed to help you lift and separate the ribs.

4. Continue separating the ribs from the belly meat, applying steady pressure as you go.

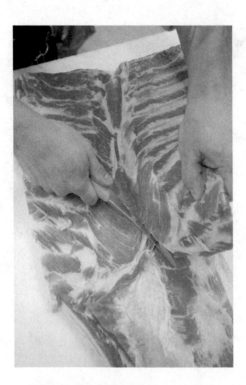

5. As the ribs are almost completely pulled away from the belly, you can use your knife to finish the separation.

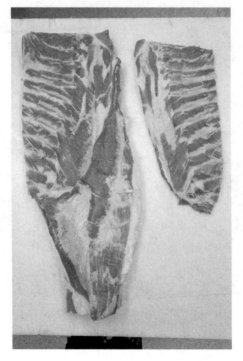

6. This is what it looks like with the ribs separated from the belly meat of the pig.

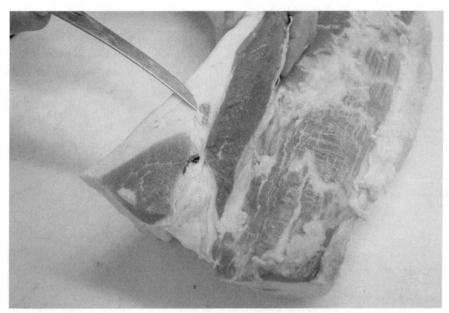

7. Locate the gland in the belly of the pig (visible in the fat at the tip of the knife). This is your marker for making the next cut.

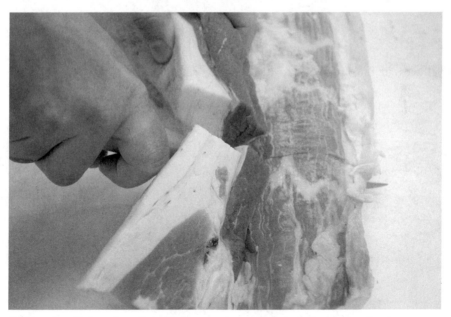

8. Square off the edge of the belly meat by cutting just above the gland area.

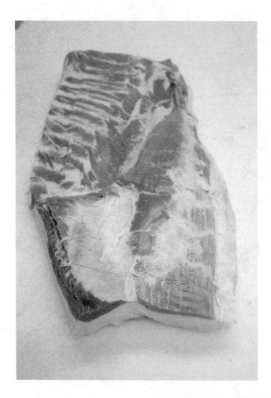

9. The belly meat has been squared off and had the ribs removed and is ready to be set aside and cured or made into bacon.

Loin and Rib Chops

Now we will separate the loin meat and then cut some delicious pork chops.

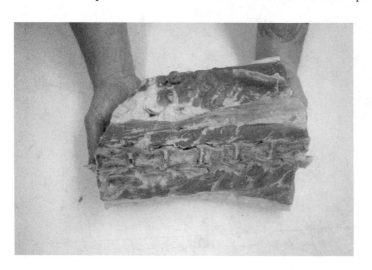

1. To cut the loin meat into juicy pork chops, you'll want to plan your thickness. Anywhere from 1 to 2 inches is usually good, and you can eyeball the width to make even cuts.

2. Use a sharp cimiter to cut the loin meat from under the last rib. This will preserve the most loin meat possible.

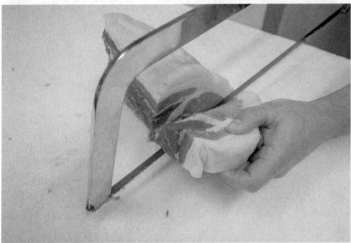

3. Cut through the meat and then bend the back away from the last rib; finish the cut with the handsaw.

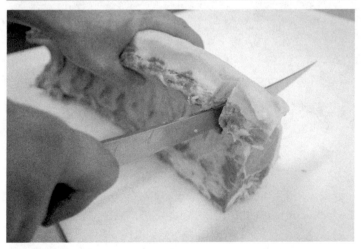

4. Cut in between the ribs with the cimiter to begin processing the rib chops. Use the knife to cut down the full length of the rib.

A CUT ABOVE

To cut the loin meat into juicy pork chops, you'll want to plan your thickness. Anywhere from 1 to 2 inches is usually good, and you can eyeball the width to make even cuts. Cutting the ribs into chops increases the number of cuts from the animal, and is one way of changing things up from what might be readily available in the grocery store.

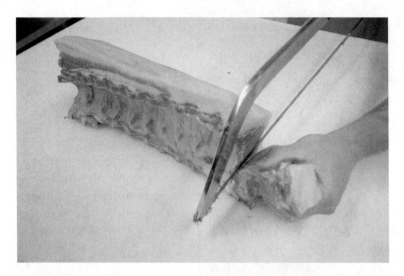

5. Open the cut by applying pressure, and use your handsaw to finish the cut. You'll cut all the way through the bone at the end to separate the rib chop from the rack.

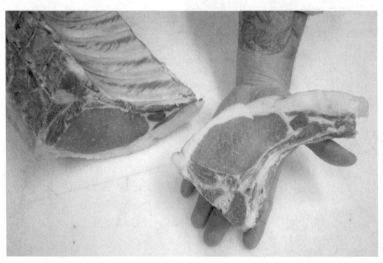

6. The final chops are the perfect size for a well-proportioned, delicious meal. They can be braised, baked, and even grilled if you're careful with the temperature.

Tenderloin and Sirloin

The sirloin is the muscle that is just above the leg. The tenderloin is a boneless cut that is removed from the inside of the loin and makes fabulous braised or grilled dishes. This tender meat is highly prized.

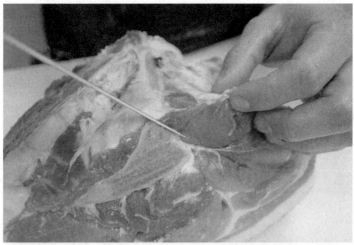

1. Follow along against the pelvic (hip) bone and begin to pull the tenderloin meat away from the sirloin. Cut down while keeping the blade against the bone, pulling gently with your fingers to expose the seam.

2. As the seam becomes exposed, pull the meat open.

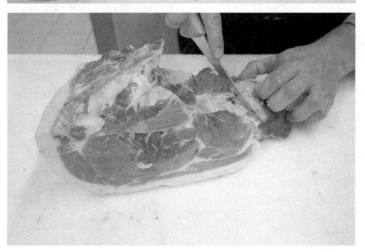

3. Continue to pull the tenderloin apart from the larger sirloin meat.

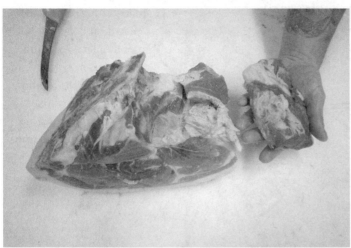

4. Use the knife as needed to assist until you've cut the tenderloin away completely. The very tender tenderloin steak is ready to wrap and freeze.

5. Remove another small steak from the other side of the pelvic bone; it is located almost directly opposite from where you removed the tenderloin. Follow the curve of the bone on the other side with your knife to start removing the steak from the sirloin.

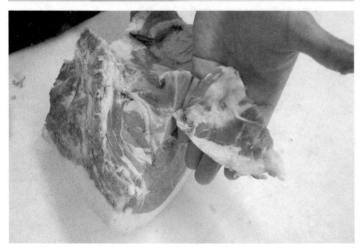

6. Cut through the flesh and separate the steak completely. This second steak should be removed from the sirloin before finishing the sirloin cuts.

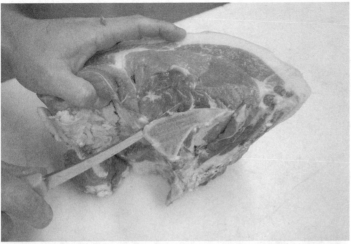

7. Remove the sirloin meat from the pelvic bone using the tip of the knife. The trick here is to work as close to the bone as possible.

8. Pull the meat away from the pelvic bone with your free hand to help you better separate the meat.

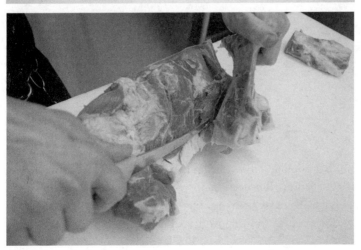

9. Finish separating the meat completely from the bone so you can create your sirloin roasts.

10. Trim the uneven edges to square up the sirloin. This will create an even and beautiful roast.

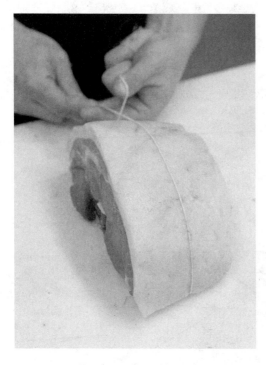

11. Fold the sirloin back and tie it tightly with butcher's twine. This will prep it as a boneless roast.

Leg of Pork

The pork leg, also known as the ham, is a popular cut for slicing into lunch meats and eating cured at Christmas dinners and other special occasions. The leg also includes the picnic, which can be used as a slow roast or turned into sausage. To make your cuts boneless, there are a few bones to remove, so sharpen those knives—we have a lot of exciting work to do!

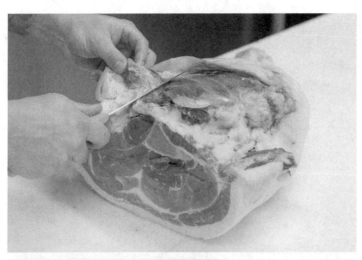

1. Locate the gland in the fat and cut it out to remove it.

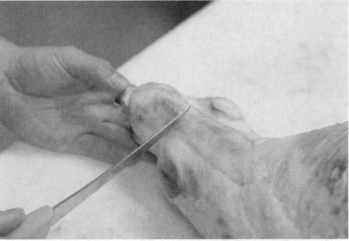

2. Square up the shank by removing the lower leg bone at the last joint.

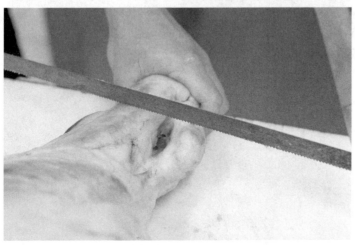

3. Finish removing the lower leg bones by using the bone saw.

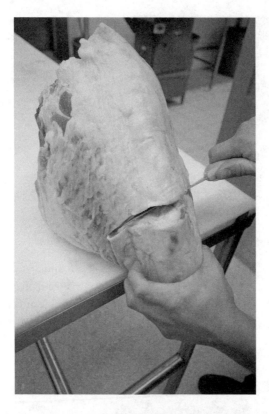

4. Feel for the joint between the shank and the leg, and use your knife to cut through the top of the leg down toward the joint. Use the edge of the counter to help expose the joint if needed.

5. Cut all the way through the leg joint with your knife by applying pressure to open the joint and remove the shank.

6. Remove the tailbone by working the knife as close to the bone as possible. Cut around the bone to remove the meat until you've completely freed the tailbone.

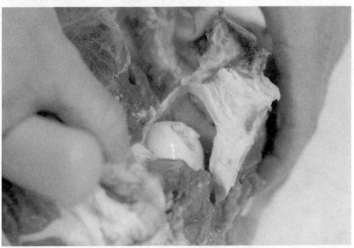

7. Cut into the top of the leg to expose the aitchbone and begin separating the meat from the bone as you cut all the way around it using the tip of your knife. It is odd shaped and can be tricky to remove.

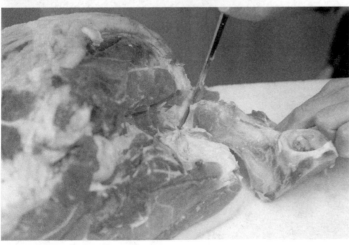

8. Stay close to the bone as you work and continue to make the cuts needed to completely remove the aitchbone.

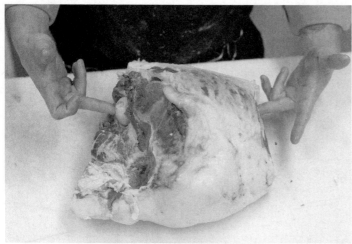

9. Now you'll be removing the femur bone from the leg. Note the location of the bone ends so you'll know the line the bone follows.

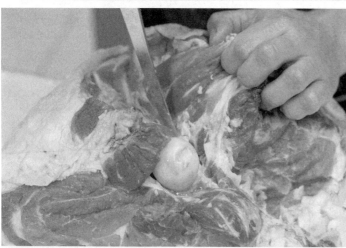

10. Cut through the top of the leg along the line of the bone to expose the top of the femur bone.

11. Once you reach the bone, you'll begin to cut the meat away from the bone. With the tip of your knife, stay as close to the bone as possible, carefully exposing it from both sides.

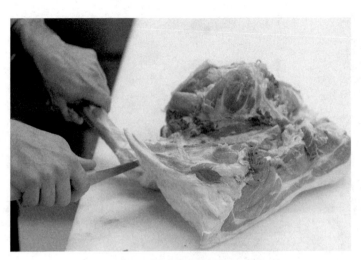

12. Once you've exposed the full length of the bone, you can start loosening one end of the bone to get it completely detached from the ham meat.

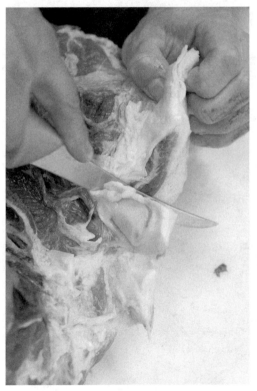

13. Next you'll want to find and remove the knee cap bone by cutting it out of the end of the meat.

14. Now that the leg is opened and boneless, butterfly the leg open along the natural seams.

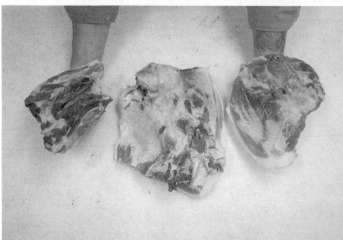

15. The leg will separate along the natural seams into three main cuts: sirloin tip, gooseneck, and inside round. These will yield large, delicious cuts.

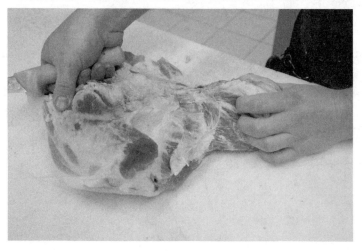

16. Pull the heel meat away from the gooseneck roast.

A CUT ABOVE

The gooseneck will make a great roast meat if you first remove the heel—a tougher muscle that requires a slower cooking method.

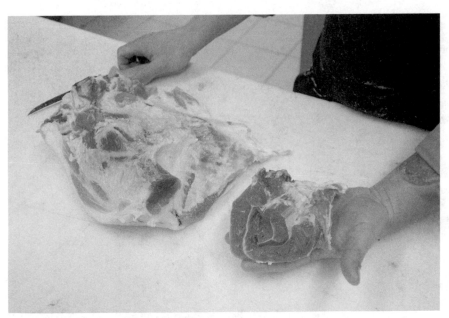

17. Use your knife to cut away the heel. Once removed, the heel meat can be ground into sausage or ground meat.

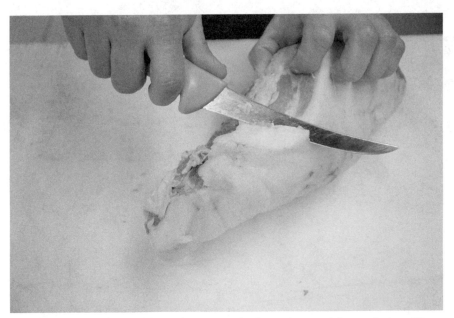

18. Remove the excess fat from the roast, which can be saved for rendering. Now your roast is finished, clean, and ready to eat!

Shoulder

The shoulder of pork contains the brisket, the picnic, and several other cuts. It can be cured on the bone like a ham or worked up into a large variety of cuts. We start by removing the foreshank and the brisket and then work up the rest of the meats from there.

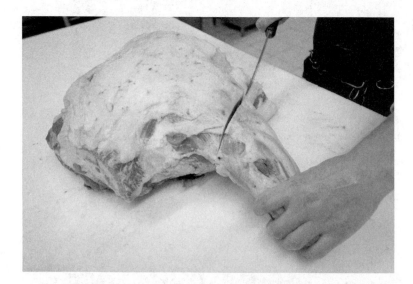

1. Cut through the flesh of the leg just above the elbow—this will be cutting through the brisket.

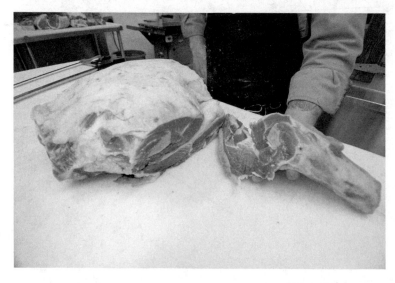

2. Once you reach the bone, use your bone saw to cut through the joint and remove the foreshank completely.

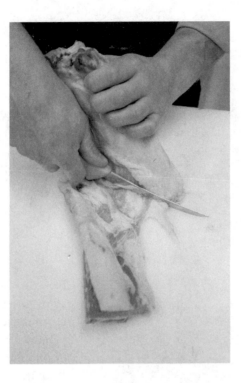

3. The brisket meat can now be cut away from the top of the foreshank, cleaned from excess fat, and then wrapped for later use.

BUTCHER'S TIP

The size of the back bones, sometimes called feather bones, will vary, but you will remove them all the same way.

4. Next we will debone the shoulder and take out the feather bones (back bones), arm bones, and shoulder blade bones. Use your knife to come up under the feather bones that lie between the neck and shoulder, working your way toward the spine.

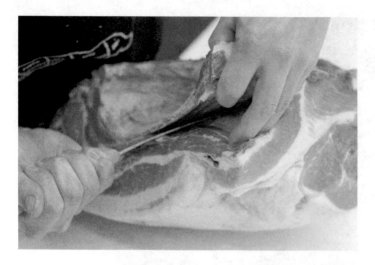

5. Work up under the three ribs left from when we cut the shoulder apart from the rib rack earlier (refer back to the first two steps of the section "Remove the Shoulder"). Take care to work under the ribs toward the spine so you can be ready to remove all the back bones.

6. Now that you've loosened all the bones, start at the top of the feather bones and pull them as you cut them free from the meat of the shoulder. Once you reach the neck end of the spine it gets a little tricky, so take your time and use your knife tip to work closely to bone, preserving as much of the meat as possible.

7. This is what the feather bones removed and discarded from the shoulder section will look like.

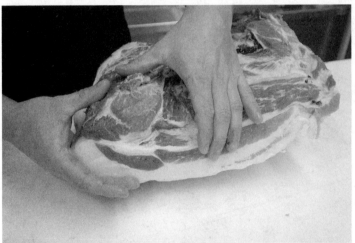

8. Now we'll be removing the *Boston*, also known as the coppa muscle, from the shoulder. The hands shows the area of the shoulder to remove.

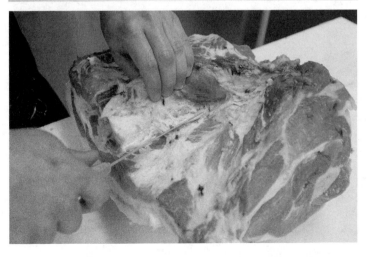

9. Find the seam two-thirds of the way in and begin working along that natural seam back toward the boston area.

A CUT ABOVE

The boston is often used in barbecue because of the thick marbling throughout, which keeps the meat juicy and flavorful during cooking.

10. When you reach the end of the blade bone, angle your cut downward to remove the boston.

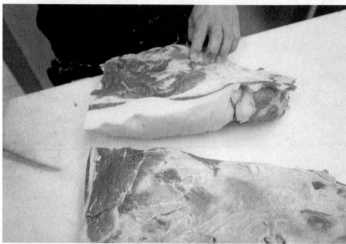

11. Once removed, the boston is a juicy and flavorful cut.

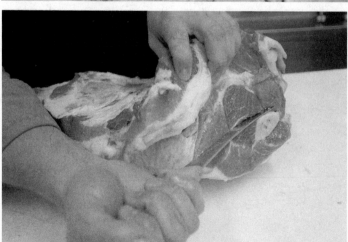

12. Next we will remove the humerus (arm bone) and shoulder blade bone. Start at the top end of the humerus and use your knife to cut along the top edge of the bone along its length.

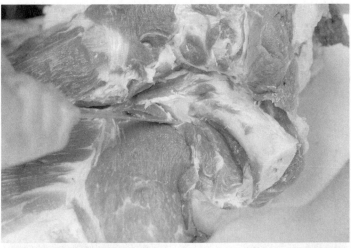

13. As you cut down the humerus bone, you will expose the blade bone. Keep cutting along the blade to detach it from the shoulder.

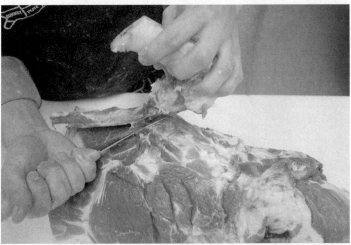

14. Cut under the humerus bone and begin to cut under the blade bone to completely free it from the shoulder meat.

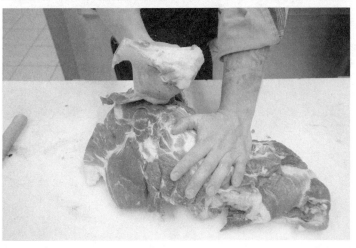

15. The shoulder blade has a spine on the backside, so you'll need to work underneath the blade on both sides to completely free it. Lift the bones away from the shoulder and cut away any final attachments as needed.

The picnic can be cured as a ham, while the boston makes excellent pulled pork barbecue. The rest of the shoulder can become a roast or ground for sausage … there are so many possibilities for cooking pork! There's a reason pork is a favored meat for barbecue, grilling, and braising. Once you begin experimenting with producing your own cuts at home, you'll be able to personalize the meat you want for the cooking you prefer!

Poultry ∞ 6

One of the most common sources of meat in North America is chicken. For the home butcher, poultry represents one of the easiest sources of meat because the livestock is easy to keep in a relatively small space and is small enough to be processed in a small kitchen.

Chicken is a popular meat for good reason—it is able to be used in a wide variety of flavorful dishes. The meat is also naturally lean, making it a great option for those with health concerns.

Introducing the Animal

This chapter demonstrates an easy way to cut up the bird so you aren't trying to roast a full carcass, à la Thanksgiving supper, every time you want to enjoy some chicken. While the photos in this chapter demonstrate a normal-size chicken, the principles are generally the same for other poultry. Chicken, duck, geese, turkey, and pheasant are all common animals that can be raised for farm-fresh meat right from your backyard.

We will start with a whole chicken, which can be simply tied if you want to freeze the whole bird. Then the next section continues on with the main breakdown of quartering the bird.

a. neck + back b. thigh c. wing d. breast e. leg

To tie a chicken, you'll need the chicken to be unfrozen, so it is pliable. You'll also need to have your butcher's twine close at hand.

1. Cut a 3½-foot-long length of string, and tuck the wings and legs in close to the bird. Place the string under the chicken at the level of the breastbone. Center it with even lengths on each side of the chicken.

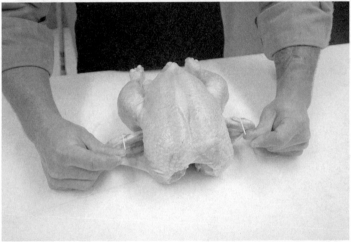

2. Loop the string around the wing tips of the chicken.

3. Guide the strings along the side of the chicken, along the inside of the thigh. This will tuck the wings close to the body of the chicken.

4. Loop the strings around the end of the drumsticks.

5. Keep the string tight, bringing both ends of the string up to the top of the bird, pulling the drumsticks and everything close together.

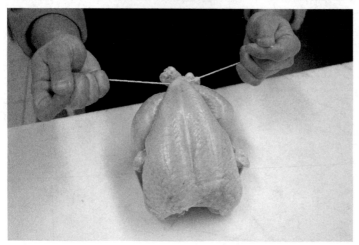

6. Tie a knot securely at the drumsticks and pull it taut to create a tightly bound chicken. Make sure the wings and legs are both pulled in tight.

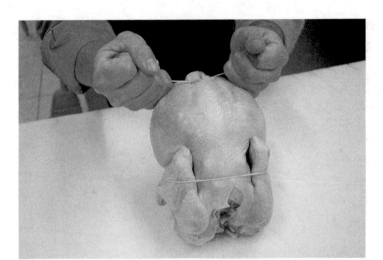

7. Turn the chicken over and use the tailbone of the chicken to tie a final knot, securing the chicken tightly to make it ready for cooking.

This is a perfect way to slow-roast a whole bird. But sometimes you don't need or want your bird whole. Breaking out the individual cuts of the bird will allow faster cooking times and a greater variety of dishes.

The Main Breakdown

Quartering a chicken doesn't take very much time at all, once you have the process down. This chapter describes a simple and common way to break down the chicken, suitable for the home butcher, and will create a variety of usable cuts for you: wings, legs, and breasts.

As with any of the animals in this book, there are more ways to process the meat than what we will be able to show. But once you get the basic steps down described here, you'll be able to build upon your skills and experiment with more advanced techniques.

Remove the Wings

The goal with the cuts that remove the wings is to preserve as much of the breast meat as possible.

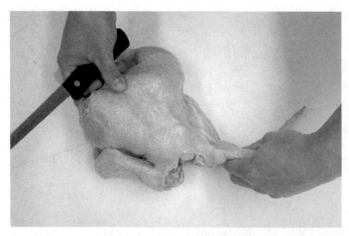

1. Hold the wing apart from the body of the chicken to gain access to the area where the cut will be made.

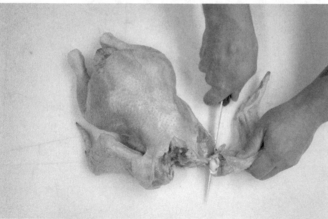

2. Score the meat to expose the joint.

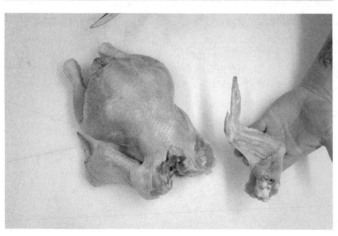

3. Use your knife to cut completely through the joint and remove the wing. Notice how the breast meat is left on the bird when the wing is removed.

Wings cooked in barbecue sauce with blue cheese dip is a classic snack for sporting events. There may not be a lot of meat on each individual wing, but they taste great and are fun to eat.

Remove the Legs

The legs of the chicken are usually considered a popular piece for children, but plenty of adults enjoy the "drumstick" as well.

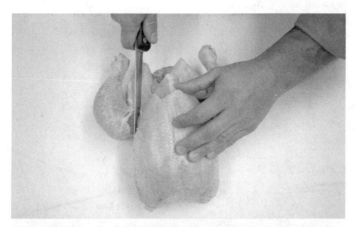

1. Make a cut through the skin of the bird, where the thigh joint is. This will keep it from ripping when you remove the thighs later.

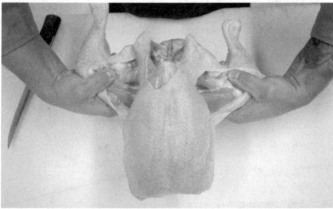

2. Grab the thighs of the chicken and open them away from the body of the bird. Pull back to open the joint of the thighs by simply popping them out of joint.

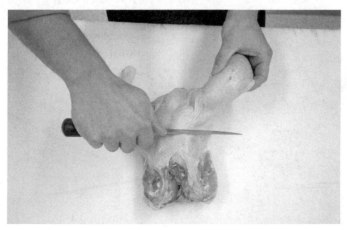

3. Now lay the chicken breast-bone down and look for the two oysters—the round bulges in the back area—about midway down the spine.

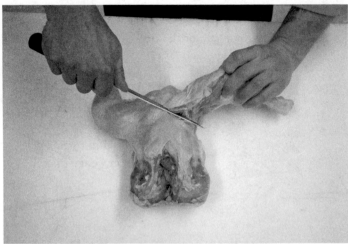

4. Cut through the skin at the top of the thigh and around the oysters. Make your cut in a half-circle motion to remove the most thigh meat possible.

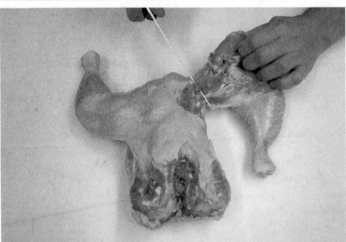

5. Use your knife to cut through the thigh joint you popped open earlier, moving as close to the spine as possible to finish the cut and remove the chicken leg.

6. Take as much meat from the back as possible when you remove the thigh from the bird.

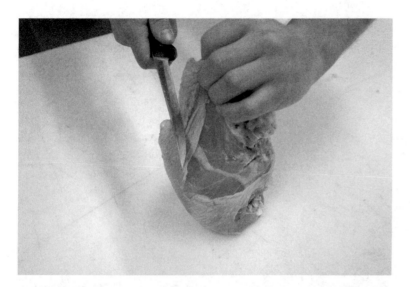

7. Remove the leftover back area by cutting the thin skin on both sides of the bird into the back section.

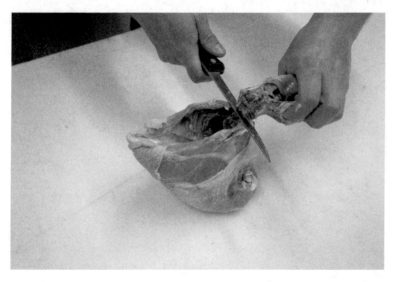

8. Pull the back section over and cut through the back joint and remove the spine. The back bones can be boiled to make a delicious and hearty soup stock.

Chicken legs can be breaded and baked, fried, or oven roasted in a savory sauce. The possibilities are practically endless.

Fillet the Breast

The breast is the part of the bird that most people are familiar with. Chicken breasts are one of the favorite options for those who are counting calories because of the lean white meat they contain.

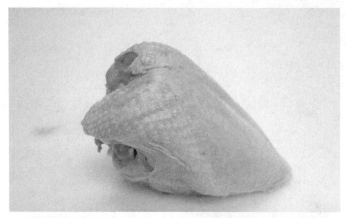

1. After removing the wings and legs, you're left with the greatest amount of meat possible. Now you'll be able to fillet the breasts off the rest of the chicken carcass.

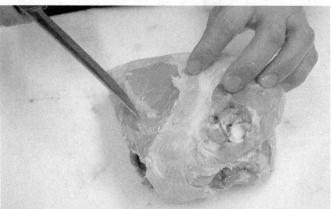

2. Position your knife right at the center line of fat on the side of the bird and make an incision to the bone.

3. Pull the breast away from the bone as you make small incisions, where needed, to gently remove the breast from the bone.

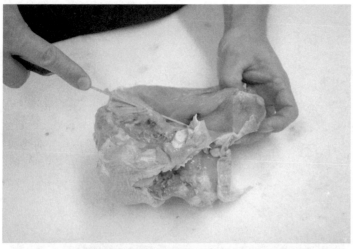

4. Follow the bones of the chest carefully with your knife. Cut the meat away from the ribs, wishbone, and finally the keel bone.

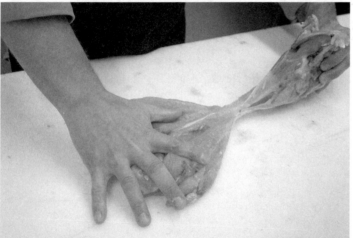

5. Repeat this on the other side of the bird, carefully peeling the breast meat away from the keel bone. It will come off in one large, heart-shaped chunk of meat. Discard the bones for stock.

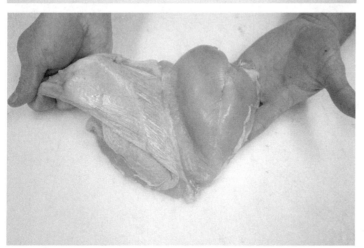

6. Remove the skin from the breast meat. You may need to use your knife where the thick attachments are in the middle.

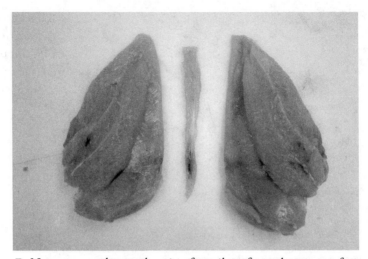

7. Now cut out the tough strip of cartilage from the center of the breasts, dividing them into two, ready-to-eat chicken breast pieces as you do so.

Moist, slow cooking keeps chicken breasts tender while giving you many options for meal additions.

Fish ∿ 7

The United States is the third largest country for fish and seafood consumption and is fortunate to have large bodies of water where hobbyists can harvest their own fish. Fish is considered an important part of a healthy diet because of the high levels of omega-3 fatty acids and low overall fat levels. If no camping trip is complete without a fishing trip to the lake, the home butcher will be the best suited to making good use of what is caught.

For many fishermen, the catching of the fish is the easiest thing. And for far too many, the only thing. Don't throw away free meat when a few simple cuts can make edible, delicious fillets for your household.

Cleaning the Animal

Though you may already know how to clean a fish, we thought we would provide a refresher course, or a "first course" for those who have never cleaned a fish.

1. Take your filleting or boning knife (either will work here) and insert approx ¼-inch to ½-inch of the blade into the vent or near the tail of the fish. You'll be running the tip portion of your knife towards the head taking care not to damage any of the insides.

2. Run your knife through to and past the area where the pelvic fins are. These are the fins that are paired up on the belly of the fish. Keep making your incision all the way to the base of the jaw of the fish.

3. On smaller fish you'll be able to grab the insides with your hand at the base of the head and simply pull them all out in one motion. Larger fish may require you to cut as you go; just watch where your fingers are as you don't want to lose one.

4. Rinse the fish thoroughly with cold water to ensure all blood and insides have been removed.

Keep in mind that fish doesn't store for a long time in the freezer. Three to six months is the maximum before flavor begins to be lost. And as with other meats, oxygen is the enemy.

Making the Cuts

The cuts on a fish are, of course, much smaller than those you see with a larger animal such as a sheep or pig. Just adjust the length of your cuts according to the size of the fish you're working with. Here the photos are taken using a salmon, which gives you a good size for visualizing the cuts being made. The salmon was purchased whole but already cleaned, so we will start with the cuts necessary to produce two delicious fillets.

1. Start with a whole fish, already gutted; it can be filleted out with just a few easy cuts.

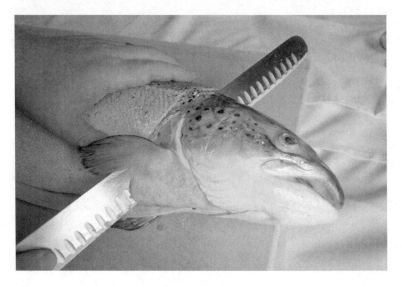

2. Find the collar right behind the gill of the fish and push your knife in until you reach the spine.

3. Twist your knife sidewise so that it lays along the top of the spine.

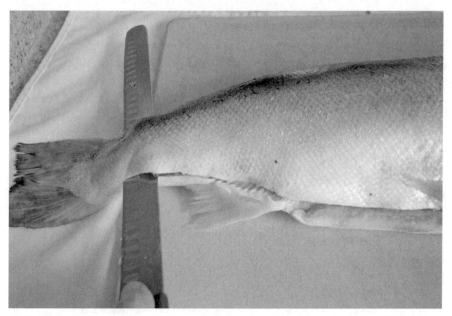

4. Pull the knife all the way through, following along the spine. Cut all the way under the meat to the tail to free the first fillet.

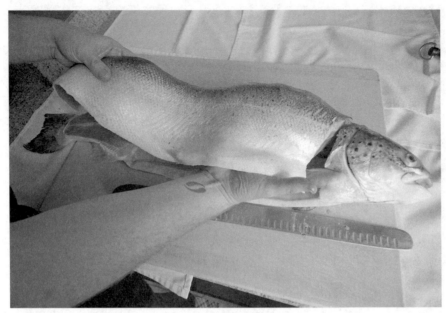

5. Use care moving the top fillet to avoid breaking the meat.

6. Put your knife back to the place behind the head where you made your first cut and work the blade between two vertebrae of the spine. Push downward until you are through the spine—it will feel like a little pop.

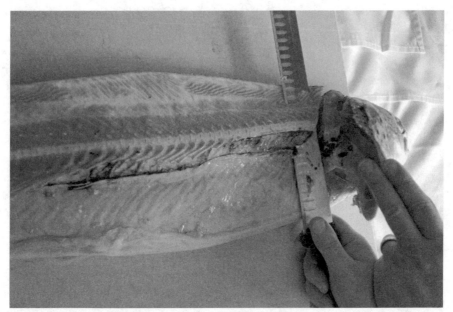

7. Turn the knife blade and remove the spine and bits of the rib off the bottom fillet.

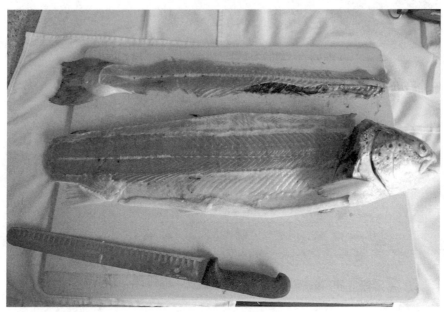

8. Cut under the spine all the way down the length of the fish and remove the tail in one piece.

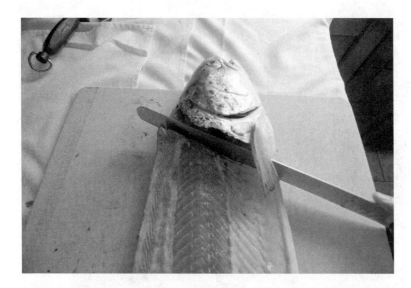

9. Remove the head with a final cut behind the gills where you started. Cut the head off on the same line that you used to cut out the fillet and spine. Watch out for the bottom fin.

10. Turn your fillet and remove the line of fat from the edges of the fillet to clean up the fish.

A CUT ABOVE

Salmon is a fatty fish, and the fat will turn black when it is cooked and be much stronger in taste, so remove as much as you prefer for your home butchery.

11. Remove the bottom trim, working under the rib bones to remove them.

12. If there is a line of cartilage remaining from where you removed the spine, cut that off the middle of the fillet.

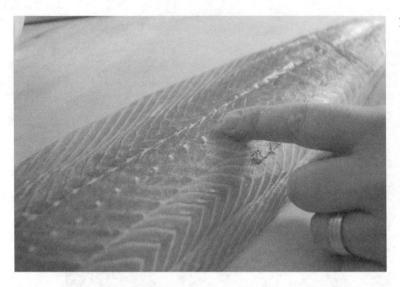

13. Brush the fillet with your fingers against the grain to help find and lift the pin bones. The bones run toward the head diagonally, so if you run your hands along the fillet moving toward the tail, the bones will gently pop up. Taking off all the pin bones is important in finishing the fillet.

14. Pull each pin bone from the fillet with sturdy tweezers, needle nose pliers, or dedicated pin-boning pliers. Remember to work gently so you don't remove too much flesh from the fillet in the process.

Many fishermen will invest in a home-use vacuum seal machine to help eliminate air from their fish fillets before freezing. Another system for eliminating air contact with the fish fillets is to coat each fish fillet with water and freeze it flat on a cookie sheet before bagging it up or wrapping it up in the freezer. In the fridge, fillets are only good for two days before they lose flavor.

Rabbit ❦ 8

Rabbit must be the most underused, underrated meat animal in North America. Its meat, whether reared humanely or slaughtered in the wild, is succulent and flavorful. Prepared by either stewing (an older rabbit), roasting (usually approx 10 weeks of age) or boned out, ground, and made into patties, rabbit's versatility is huge.

Rabbit can be a great way to add quality, organic, and humanely processed meat to your freezer. For families on a budget, it can be a huge boon. For the home butcher, the opportunity to try your hand on rabbit means you are free to learn and experiment and find your knife skills without the pressure of having spent hundreds of dollars on a large animal.

If you're lucky enough to either be a hunter or know someone who hunts, then you're one step closer to enjoying the bounty of this fine little creature. In this situation, you should be able to secure a healthy, wild rabbit that offers a deeper flavor profile and presents you with the opportunity to skin and butcher it for a favorable amount of money. Harvest a healthy population of rabbits in season to fill your freezer with a supply enough for a few months at least.

Cleaning the Animal

Unlike chicken, fish, or other small animals available to the home butcher, most rabbits are sourced whole and intact, necessitating their skinning and cleaning. Cleaning a rabbit really couldn't be easier. Much like with chicken, you can cook the animal whole or piece it out.

The following steps will show you how it can be done inside on a counter or over a table.

1. Hang the rabbit by its hind legs on a nail or screw through the gambrel (the thick tendon on the rear of the leg, just above the foot).

2. Make an incision with a sharp knife around both hind legs just below where you've hung it to cut through the skin.

3. Free up a bit of skin around the hind legs so you have enough to get a good grip with your index finger and thumb.

4. At this point you should be able to pull the skin off with minimal effort all the way down to the head.

5. Now you can choose to either cut the head off or free the skin from the head with your knife. It has always seemed easiest to cut through the neck bones and remove the head.

6. Now make an incision from the anus to the chest cavity to remove the innards.

7. Pull down gently on the anus, taking care not to puncture the intestines.

8. Release the thin membrane that attaches the stomach to the kidneys with your fingers in order separate the two and allow for the kidneys, heart, and liver to remain intact.

9. Put the offal in a plastic bag and then directly into the refrigerator for further use.

10. Once all the entrails have been removed, rinse the inside and out with cold water.

Now that your whole rabbit is skinned, it is ready for butchering. Rabbit, like other meats, should be kept in the fridge at under 40°F. Rabbit will store in the fridge for two days or can be frozen for long-term storage. Cooking temperatures should reach 160°F on your meat thermometer when preparing your savory rabbit dishes.

Making the Cuts

Lucky for the home butcher, you will most likely only be able to find whole rabbits at the grocer or butcher. This means you'll get the chance to do some basic butchery to get the rabbit into more manageable cuts, should you wish, that is. Rabbits are just fine roasted whole, but breaking down a rabbit is a cinch.

A CUT ABOVE

When buying a whole rabbit, look for color. Similarly to pork, rabbit raised in captivity can appear almost gray with too much moisture. You'll want a nice pink color and a firm texture. Remember these animals, left to their own devices, are runners; therefore, their meat will be naturally firm.

You'll want to separate the carcass just behind the front haunches, and again at the rear legs. This will give you the three primals.

1. The front legs are not attached bone to bone, so you can cut up from the "armpit" area with a sharp knife to detach the front legs. Removing the front legs with a chef's knife will give you the force needed to cut them off completely.

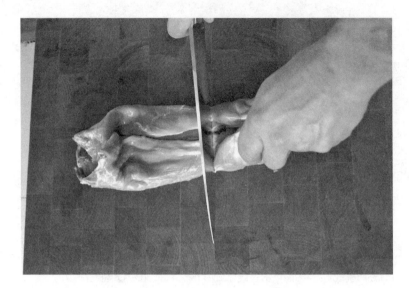

2. Lay the rabbit on its back and grasp the back legs firmly. Press the knife through the middle of the hips of the rabbit to cut the hip section in half with your knife. There are joints in the spine that allow for easier access.

BUTCHER'S TIP

As with chicken, the back legs are often a prized portion of the rabbit. In fact, the meaty hind legs can make up about 40 percent of the rabbit's total meat yield.

3. Now cut between the legs, making two separate but equal pieces. The loin section will need to have all the silver skin cleaned off it. If the ribs are still attached to this section, cut them off using a cleaver or kitchen shears and also add to the stew pot.

4. Grasp the loin in both hands and force a break down the ribs. This will most likely happen to one side, which is just fine. Cutting the loin in half will make more manageable pieces for use in braises.

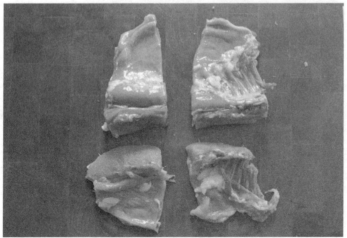

5. Now split the loin and rib section apart. Cut with a cleaver or sturdy knife to split where the tenderloin ends and ribs begin. Now your rabbit is in parts manageable to cook.

The boneless meat of the belly section is tender and can be cured, made into jerky, or other preparations, depending on your mood. These more tender pieces on the animal also make very good quick-frying or grilling cuts.

Butchering Beyond the Cuts 3

What you see in the grocery store is just the beginning of what you can create at home. Tailor your gourmet meats with the flavors and seasonings that you prefer. Learn how to make sausage, bacon, jerky, and other meat items from your home butchery work.

Charcuterie: Curing and Brining

9

Much like the role of the butcher in years gone by, the role of the *charcutiers* was and is a much highly touted profession. Guilds were even developed with strict methods and procedures created in order to maintain a high level of quality and consistency.

Charcuterie (French: *chair* "flesh" and *cuit* "cooked" means literally pork butcher) is a method for food preparation generally involving salt to "cook" the flesh, allowing it to preserve the meat for later consumption. First developed as a way to prolong the animals' abundance over the cold months when food was scarce, charcuterie has since turned into a global food industry on its own. The home butcher needs only very basic equipment, proper storage, and time in order to achieve some tasty products.

Charcuterie can be made from most animals that the home butcher would be working with; beef, chicken, duck, lamb, and especially pork all lend themselves exceptionally well to further processing. On top of the products that are more well known, such as bacon, prosciutto, and ham, there is a plethora of options that can expand your culinary palate.

Items such as rillettes, pâtés, and head cheese add new dimensions of flavor. Better yet, these techniques are something that can be put together without much fuss at a beginner's level. Once you get a handle on the basic techniques of these home butchery add-ons, the only limit in how you adapt and master this craft becomes your creativity!

Fermented and Salt-Cured Meats

There's a good mix of science and practical wisdom (of experts in the field) that makes this art form really shine. Much like baking, you have certain precise measurements that need to be followed, but there is also a hand's on, creative feel for the process and knowing the environment in which these types of meats are cured.

Bacteria play an important role in the outcome as well. Too hot, and the meat will spoil or develop bacteria that could cause serious illness. Too cool, and the bacteria won't be in the proper conditions to thrive. It's really a fight for the artisan to control his or her environment and promote the growth of beneficial bacteria (the ones that encourage fermentation), improve flavor, lower the pH level by increasing the acidity, and encourage mold growth (highly desired in certain Italian salamis).

Thankfully, there are ways to combat the enemies. Adding salt and nitrates/nitrites aid in drawing moisture out of the meat, which is similar to dry-aging beef. It also aids in eliminating the possibility of botulism. One could also smoke the meat in question to bring the cured item outside of the food danger zone (40–140°F). However, more often than not we are looking for unsmoked results.

The History of Bacon

Bacon is North America's holy grail of charcuterie. No other food receives so much attention. It's being infused with cocktails, deconstructed in recipes, baked with, made into chocolate bars, and generally obsessed over by food professionals and home chefs alike. The appeal is simple: a salty, fatty, smoky, rich, and somewhat tender piece of meat.

Bacon is usually cured pig belly (at least in North America) and is cooked and either enjoyed on its own or paired with so many flavor combinations it's staggering. Bacon is quite simply an easy food to cook with, as it's very forgiving and also gives so much back to whatever you've added it to.

Bacon's history coincides with the birth of charcuterie, whereas the belly was salted for preservation. This was the beginning of salt pork, which is a very popular item still seen in the United Kingdom, Ireland, and North America to flavor beans or vegetables when boiled in water. It wasn't until much later (approximately the seventeenth century) that we see folks smoking the belly, shoulder, and loins of pigs, which we now refer to as bacon.

Certain pig breeds lend themselves better to bacon than others. Yorkshires and Tamworth are the breeds of choice, given their lean and long carcasses. Tamworth pigs are a favored breed for homemade bacon.

Making Bacon

Making your own bacon at home provides the home butcher with, again, a wealth of opportunity with flavor combinations and options as to how your bacon will be used: cooked with breakfast, enjoyed on burgers, braised for a rich appetizer, the list goes on and on. And making bacon couldn't be easier. Whether you choose to simply salt the belly and hang it in a cool climate (pancetta) or smoke it for the all-familiar smoked variety, bacon, when done properly, is a rewarding and somewhat easy project that can yield fantastic results.

A CUT ABOVE

When making bacon, be sure to use kosher salt as opposed to other types. It is easier to mix, and the large granules pull moisture from the belly much better than, for example, table salt.

The process is the same for making both pancetta and bacon. You will need the following:

1 pork belly (rind on)   ½ cup of brown sugar
½ cup of kosher salt

You will also need either a sizable container, a large sealable plastic bag, or enough cling wrap to wrap the belly a few times over.

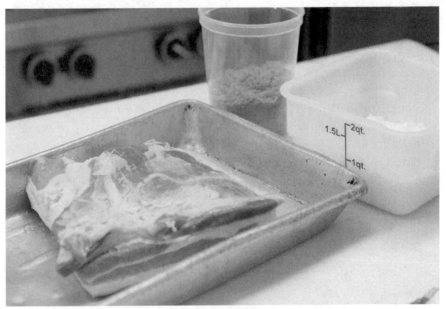

1. Gather your salt, sugar, and seasonings (some bacon recipes may call for additional spices for a specific flavor). Combine thoroughly to ensure that everything is evenly mixed.

2. Apply your salt/sugar/spice mix and rub it all over the pork belly in a nonreactive container. Take care to make sure the entire belly is rubbed with the cure. Either wrap the pork belly in several layers of cling wrap or securely cover it in its container. Place it in the refrigerator or a cool area what won't exceed 35–38°F. Any warmer and you could be inviting bacterial growth. After 5 days, flip the bacon over, and then once another 5 days have elapsed, you're done! Well, almost.

3. Remove the belly and rinse it under cold water for as long as it takes to remove the entire cure. Place the bacon on some paper towels and pat dry. You can now choose either to smoke the bacon (option 1) or hang the rolled, cleaned belly in a cool climate to air dry (option 2).

4. Option 1: Put the non-rolled belly in a smoker at 170°F until the internal temperature reaches 150°F. Voilà, bacon. Option 2: Carefully roll the cured belly so that it is even in thickness. Tie the strings at even intervals to make sure it's as tight as possible. Hang your tied pork belly for 4 to 6 weeks at no warmer than 40 degrees. You'll know it's ready when it's hard but has a slight give when squeezed.

Using Nitrates

Sodium nitrate added to your curing mix will do four beneficial things to your meat:

- Provide a nice pinkish color
- Add a sharp, distinct flavor
- Virtually eliminate the opportunity for botulism to develop
- Prevent the fats from going rancid

On the downside, an over-consumption of sodium nitrate or sodium nitrate can lead to an increased risk of cancer. The United States Department of Agriculture (USDA) has developed regulations regarding the legal quantities that producers can add to cured meats, and as a result, the actual connection between cancer and said products is virtually nonexistent. No doubt this is a very divisive topic and one that needs to be addressed.

More and more often you are seeing nitrate-free products that make the claim of having no sodium nitrates added. These products, however, usually use additives such as celery juice or celery powder, which both contain very high quantities of naturally occurring nitrates.

It's been noted that since we regularly ingest nitrates through a daily intake of everyday foods that, if they were cancer-causing, our bodies would have some major flaws present. If you feel comfortable using them, please source out well-trusted recipes and follow them faithfully, as the amounts they suggest hopefully have been tested to be safe. You may also feel more comfortable with naturally sourced nitrates like those found in celery powder.

Brining

Submerging meat into a salt and sugar brine with other aromatics can create some interesting flavors. The meat itself becomes more moist and tender in the end result. Salt works double duty in the brining process, adding a salty flavor to the meat and providing moisture to the meat's cells for hydration via osmosis.

The amount of time to brine a particular type of meat is at the cook's discretion, but it's generally based on the size of the meat and the concentration of the brine mix. For example, a large turkey may be left in overnight, while a smaller pork roast may only need a few hours.

A basic brine consists of, but is not limited to, the following:

> 1.5 cups kosher salt
>
> 1.5 cups brown sugar
>
> 8 liters of cold water

All ingredients are then brought to a boil on a stove until the salt and sugar dissolve. Once this happens, remove the brine from the heat and allow it to cool to room temperature. Once cooled slightly, place it in a refrigerator and chill. Your brine is now ready to use.

Making Corned Beef

Corned beef is a great example of how a brine works its magic. The curing salts preserve the pink hue and impart that savory flavor, while the pickling spices in the brine impart the flavors of the spice and maintain a high level of retainable moisture.

The following is a suggested brine you can use with a 4 to 6 pound piece of beef brisket:

1½ gallons water	1 TB. red pepper flakes
1 lb. brown sugar	3 cloves garlic
3 lb. kosher salt	4 fresh bay leaves
1 TB. whole peppercorns	3 TB. pink salt (this is optional, but
1 TB. juniper berries	it will give your corned beef that
1 TB. thyme	distinct deep red hue)
2 TB. mustard seeds	

1. Add all brine ingredients to a large stock pot and stir well over a low heat until all the salt, brown sugar, and pink salt have dissolved.

2. Bring the mixture to a boil for a few minutes before removing it from the heat and allow it to cool completely.

3. Place the brisket in a nonreactive container with a lid or foil to cover. Add the cool brine to the brisket and brine for 5 to 7 days.

4. Rinse the meat fully under cold water before cooking.

5. Bring the brisket to a boil, then cover and reduce heat to a simmer for 3 to 4 hours. You can add any seasonings and extra vegetables you'd like at this point—carrots, onions, celery, and garlic are the most common. If you were to smoke it at this point instead of simmering, you would make pastrami. Brisket requires a long low heat, so check your smoker direction booklet for suggestions but expect at least 3 to 5 hours at under 300°F.

Curing Poultry

The same principles for brining pork and beef are at work in the brining of poultry, although pickling spices are omitted in favor of aromatics like juniper berries, peppercorns, star anise—basically any citrus and/or fresh herbs. Placing a roasting chicken or turkey in a properly seasoned brine will always add a preseasoned flavor and help maintain moisture in a dry, hot oven.

Make sure you either allow the bird to air dry thoroughly or pat it down with paper towels before you roast it. Also, monitoring your time is of the essence, as too much time in a brine can work against you by breaking down the fibers in the meat, creating a somewhat mushy texture.

Here's a good general guideline to work with:

1 chicken; 4 lb. whole	4 to 12 hours
1 chicken; cut in pieces	1 to 1.5 hours
1 turkey; 12–15 lb. whole	16 to 24 hours
1 turkey breast; bone-in or boneless	3 to 6 hours
1 Cornish game hen	3 to 6 hours

Once you've brined your meat you are ready to put the turkey straight into the oven or smoker. Your meat will be more tender and flavorful than you may be used to if you've never brined your meat before.

Forcemeats: Sausages and More

10

Forcemeats are a combination of meat, ground or chopped, mixed with fats. This is where sausages, pates, rillettes, terrines, and emulsified sausages come into play.

Sausages are made by putting seasoned ground meats into a casing, natural or synthetic, (sometimes) twisting them into links, and utilizing various cooking methods. In addition, there are two types of sausages: cooked and raw. Cooked sausages are warmed or smoked during production to allow them to be eaten immediately after they are made. Raw sausages are simply not cooked after they are prepared.

Pates are a finer textured mixture of meat, offal, and fat, seasoned, then put into specific molds and allowed to "set up" in a cooler environment. Some pates are further emulsified with creams to form a moose-like consistency.

Rillettes are done in a similar fashion to pates. However, rillettes are left with a more coarse texture as opposed to pates and terrines, which are made into a paste-like consistency.

Terrines are done in a similar fashion to pates. Generally they are not ground but instead are left in larger pieces and mixed with fat and heavy seasonings. As both terrines and pates are eaten cold, the seasoning becomes very important. You will use more seasonings for the cold dishes because cooler temperatures subdue the flavors.

Emulsified sausages are cooked sausages that have combined meat, fat, and spices and made into a paste-like consistency. They are generally smoked or cooked in a moist heat after being encased in either a natural or synthetic casing. Most notable to the emulsified sausage family are hot dogs, bologna, and mortadella. Similarly, you'll see liver sausages and some pates/terrines handled with the same treatment.

The Origination of Sausage

Sausage was created out of necessity. When a family or families decided to slaughter a hog, they wanted to use it *all*, and nothing was to be wasted. For example:

- Head and *trotters* (feet) can be rendered down and covered in *aspic* (leftover liquid after making headcheese).

- Fat can be rendered down for either a cooking oil or used as lard for baking.

- Skin can be left on the desired cut for texture as "cracklin".

- Edible muscles can be consumed.

- Heart, liver, and kidneys can be consumed.

- Bones can be boiled for stock.

The only part of the animal left is the intestines. Eventually it was discovered that the intestines could be used as a natural meat encasement. Once properly cleaned, fresh meats could be seasoned, prepared, and forced into them. Sometimes they were eaten raw and other times allowed to hang in cool, dark areas and dehydrate over the winter. This provided families with meat over the cooler months.

Sources point to this discovery of using intestines for natural casing to be somewhere in Italy or Spain, but proper records were never kept on such things at the time. It's clearly prevalent in both Italian and Spanish cooking and their curing of such fantastic meats, so it's really splitting hairs at this point to argue the improvable. However sausage came to be, we are eternally grateful it did!

Ordering Your Sausage Meats

Be particular when you order your meat. Heritage breeds such as Berkshire and Tamworth will be better suited for sausages because of fat content, but you could just as easily have your butcher grind you some pork shoulder for sausages if a grinder isn't available. Be very particular when you get your meat. Pork shoulder is a great place to start as it has high fat content.

When you're talking sausage, you're talking fat. This is no place to find lean substitutes. While chicken, turkey, and every other type of meat can be made into sausage, there's always an underlying theme: adding fat. It's what's going to make the sausage edible and decadent, it bastes the meat while cooking, and it adds that creamy texture every sausage enthusiast loves.

Sausage-Making Equipment

Modern home butchery has made the art of sausage-making both fun and easy for all levels of skill. Home-sized grinders and sausage stuffers are all easily accessible through some hardware stores, and natural casings can be sought in most small, independent butcher shops or Italian grocers.

Meat Grinder

This will make the job so much easier. There are now small appliances that come with meat grinder and sausage stuffer attachments. Your other option is a tabletop grinder. These come in all shapes and sizes but are generally reserved for the serious meat enthusiast as they're priced accordingly.

Grinders are more flexible when allowing you to choose your meat texture. Plates, as they're known, are available in different *dies* (sizes), from very course to extremely fine. Make sure you're getting the one best suited for your sausage making needs. When doing large quantities of meat and sausage, a grinder will definitely expedite the process. And with a low-cost purchase of a sausage nozzle, this makes casing sausages a snap!

Sausage Stuffer

This is a tabletop appliance that is essentially a cylinder and a piston that pushes the meat to a spout with a nozzle. There's a split in opinion of whether these are a luxury item or a necessity.

Casings

Hog, lamb, and beef casings are all available, but you should be aware of the job at hand before purchasing your natural casings. They can be expensive due to the rigorous cleaning that takes place in order for them to be considered food safe. Pork intestines are the most often used for today's popular sausages. Lamb intestines make great breakfast sausages, while beef intestines are great for larger items such as bologna, capacola, mortadella, or larger salamis.

There are synthetic casings that are available, but I suggest staying with what Mother Nature has provided. Natural is easier to work with and allows for a small margin of error when filling them with meat. Be sure to soak your casings in lukewarm water for at least 20 minutes before using them. When you're ready to begin, rinse the casings again and add them to a new batch of fresh lukewarm water. As you go, make sure you're allowing the clean water to pass through the casings before you put them on the nozzle.

Scale

Weighing your ingredients is essential and shouldn't be left to chance. It'll be the reason why your sausages turn out either bland, way too salty, or over seasoned. Start by finding some tested recipes from trusted sources and then adapt to your tastes from there.

There's no shortage of scales for sale these days. From digital to mechanical, there's a scale to fit your needs and budget. As long as it's calibrated properly it will be imperative to the quality of your encased meats.

Ingredients

All too often, people who first begin sausage making get all set up with equipment but don't bother purchasing new spices—thinking the spices that have been in their cupboard for years will suffice. Please rethink this! Your dried spices should be treated much the same as your fresh ones. While dry spices will last longer, stored properly, they do still have a shelf life. Luckily for us there are bulk foods and spices available either online or at larger grocery retailers. Buy what you need to get you started; it'll be a cost worth incurring.

Making Fresh Sausage

Once you've got all your equipment in order it's time to begin making your sausages.

1. Organize all the meat that your recipe calls for. If you needs a separate amount of fat, now's the time to get it ready to go into the grinder.

2. Grind the meat into a large tub. Then, weigh out and measure all your recipe spices and soak your casings in clean lukewarm water.

3. Add the fresh and dry ingredients to your meat and mix everything together. Once you think you've mixed enough, mix more. Ingredients like coarse salt need to be evenly distributed, and there's no way to monitor this with the naked eye. Mix and mix again.

4. Now it's time to put the casings on the nozzle. Take one open end to a casing and split it apart between your index and middle finger, creating an opening in the casing. Dip the open casing in the water in which it's been soaking, taking in a good amount of water. Now use your free hand to force the water through the casing. This will flush out any salt that's been used in the cleansing process. Now gently stretch the casing over the nozzle and push the casing on until there's no more room.

BUTCHER'S TIP

If your recipe doesn't call for some other form of liquid such as wine, vinegar, beer, liquid smoke, or other cooking liquids, then you'll want to add plain water. Water will help the sausage case easier and adds a looser texture to the meat, which can be key for the sausage texture desired.

5. Casing is an acquired talent, generally a combination of the right amount of tension vs. the amount of meat that's being forced through the nozzle. Feed the spiced meat mixture through the nozzle with one hand, and with the other hand apply an ever so slight amount of pressure around the casing to allow it to fill to your desired amount.

6. At the desired sausage length, grasp the cased sausage at the twisting point between your thumb and forefinger and press down to make the crease in the casing. A 6-inch sausage is pretty standard, but you might be going for something other than the normal "bun length." Twist the length of sausages two or three times to seal each link around itself and create each sausage portion.

A CUT ABOVE

Fill the casings slowly and evenly with controlled pressure. Allow enough "wiggle room" for twisting the links. It is simpler to case an entire length of casings at one time, or as much as the nozzle can hold, before linking the sausages. Remember that an extremely tight casing will most likely yield broken links when you twist them. You want something loose enough to twist but compact enough that they'll hold their shape when cooking.

7. Once the sausages have set, you can cut the individual links apart.

A CUT ABOVE

Twisting the sausages immediately after they're cased allows for the sausages to "set up" after a day. This means the twisted casings between the links will harden without moisture building up. It will also help keep the shape of the sausage intact once they've been cut into individual links. Allowing the sausages time in the casings also lets the flavors combine and come together.

Smoking Sausages and Meats

Smoking sausages and meats is a great way to further the life of fresh meat and add a different dimension of flavor. Two different methods are associated with smoking:

- ⚜ Hot smoking—This means you're "cooking" the meat by bringing it up to a desired internal temperature of approximately 126 to 176°F and maintaining that temperature for an extended period of time. This will enable the smoke to really penetrate the meat and provide the depth of smoky flavor. Some examples of hot smoked meats include bacon, hot dogs, pulled pork, and smoked brisket.

- ⚜ Cold smoking—This is done at a temperature between 68 to 86°F, allowing the meat to take on a smoky flavor without cooking the meat. Meats such as chicken, pork, and beef are all examples of items that could be cold smoked to increase flavor potentials. Fish also takes quite well to this approach. It should be noted that food is not safe to eat after being cold smoked, unlike hot-smoked foods that have reached an edible internal temperature.

Try burning different types of wood (maple, hickory, cherry, or apple) or utilize rubs and marinades to season to impart different flavors. Often the outcome can be enhanced if you baste as you go.

Smoking Equipment

Smokers have become readily available over the years through different sources (see Appendix B). When choosing a smoker, understand that the most popular brands (The Big Green Egg, the Bradley Smoker, and the Weber Smokey Mountain) require different levels of know-how to operate. Consider whether your smoker of choice is user friendly for the beginner while providing enough variation once you become an experienced pit master. Do your research and find one that is right for your needs.

Smoking means fire, so you'll need a source for the smoke. Will you be using charcoal, hard wood pieces, or wood pellets? Each provides different outcomes and flavors for the meat, so again, choose the best for your specific needs.

A good set of tools and safety equipment will make smoking much more manageable. A sturdy apron, heavy duty oven mitts, and BBQ utensils (tongs, spatula, brush, etc.) will be needed. I'd also recommend a source for water—either a spray bottle or running water near by.

While home smokers can be found in a huge variety of shapes, sizes, and price points, they all have the same basic function: to transform your meat cuts into delicious and flavorful dishes!

BUTCHER'S TIP

A well thought out approach to how you'll be smoking will nip any complications in the bud. Choose and prepare your rub or marinade before beginning your work with the meat. Have an idea of smoking times and internal temps, and of course, the patience to deal with any unexpected occurrences.

Making Jerky

Jerky has come a long way from the initial, humble beginnings of drying strips of meat on racks over fire. Initially, like most cured meats, meat was trimmed of all visible fats and salt was added. It was then left in a warm, dry environment to dry out, thus preserving the meat for future consumption.

Today's jerky has become a household commodity. Flavors span a wide spectrum, from basic teriyaki and honey garlic to more complex flavors like Szechwan molasses and mandarin orange ginger. People are now running the gamut on proteins (types of meat) used: domestic animals such as pork, beef, and lamb as well as game meats such as caribou, elk, moose, and horse, to name but a few.

Jerky is an easy process and one that allows the home butcher a lot of flexibility when it comes to experimenting with flavors and spices. Getting the basic steps of jerky down first, as in the sample recipe here, will lay the groundwork for creative exploration. You can try your first batch of jerky right in your home oven with a simple cookie sheet.

The following is a suggested marinade recipe for homemade jerky:

1½ to 2 pounds inside round, sliced thin	2 TB. freshly ground black pepper
¾ cup Worcestershire sauce	2 tsp. onion powder
½ cup soy sauce	1 tsp. liquid smoke (optional)
1 TB. honey	1 pinch red pepper flakes

1. Combine all the marinade ingredients in a bowl and mix thoroughly.

2. Add the meat and coat it evenly with the marinade.

3. Place the coated meat and the left over marinade into a sealable plastic container or bag.

4. Let the ingredients combine in the refrigerator for up to 12 hours.

5. Remove the meat from the plastic bag and allow to drain, then pat the meat dry with paper towels.

6. You'll be drying the meat as the final stage of jerky-making.

There are a couple options for drying the meat because home butchers can use either the oven-drying method or finish their jerky in their home dehydrating machine.

If you decide to make it on a regular basis and want to branch out more, consider purchasing a dehydrator. These machines are designed to maintain 140°F and pull moisture out of the cooking chamber. While they are made for this purpose, they are slightly flawed. Because the racks are arranged top to bottom, the bottom gets more heat than the top, so it's wise to keep an eye on your progress. You can adjust the heat at the later stages or rearrange the meat to avoid overdoing your meat. When using a dehydrator, simply follow the instruction manual that comes with your unit as each will be a little different.

To finish jerky in the oven, a less expensive but more variable method, you'll need to use a little more finesse. Arrange the seasoned, thinly sliced meat in single layers on the cookie sheet, making sure not to overlap or have any edges of the meat strips touching each other. Put the arranged meat into a 250°F oven and bake for approximately 4 hours, or until they are dry to the touch. Remove from the oven and continue to dry on baking racks for 24 hours in a cool, dry place. They need good air circulation through the entire process.

While the recipe provided gives you a great basic jerky, many connoisseurs have their own "secret" recipes, and you are sure to develop your own in no time. Jerky seasoning is something of a fine art and becomes a source of individual pride. As with chili cook-offs, jerky is the stuff of legend. And who knows—the world's best jerky might next be made right in your own kitchen!

Creating Pates

Pates are a clever way for the home butcher to enjoy some of the offal that may either be discarded for the simple reason that he may not have any good uses for them. By grinding or finely chopping the liver and kidneys, mixing them with finely ground pork and a wide variety of herbs and spices, you now have a delicious way to make use of something that's often thrown in the waste bin.

A CUT ABOVE

In the early days of gastronomy in France and England there was no shortage of pate or terrine recipes, as both were used interchangeably those days. In fact, most butcheries or charcuteries had their fare share of offerings; it wasn't uncommon for each to have at least four during the week, or when gearing up for Sunday suppers or holidays, upwards to 10 different varieties to choose from.

These days there are plenty of experimentation happening within the world of pates. Chefs are adding their own unique twists on classics, from adding very expensive ingredients such as foie gras, pork tenderloins, and brandy, to the simplest of recipes with a basic ingredient list of chicken livers, butter, shallots, thyme, double cream, and salt.

Cooking methods for pate can vary from poaching the blended ingredients to sautéing them.

The following is the ingredient list for making a basic chicken liver pate:

175 g. butter, diced	75 ml. of either port or Madeira
1 tsp. thyme leave, chopped finely	75 ml. of double cream
1 shallot, chopped finely	¼ tsp. ground ginger
350 g. chicken livers, cleaned and chopped	Salt to taste

1. Heat half the butter in a warm fry pan, add the thyme and shallots, allow them to soften. Turn the stove up to a medium-high and add the chicken livers and sauté until the livers are brown on the outside but slightly pink on the inside. Pour contents into food processor.

2. Add the maderia to the pan and boil to reduce to a couple teaspoons. Pour contents into food processor then add the cream, ginger, salt and pepper, and blitz until smooth. Add half of what's left of the butter and blitz it into the mixture.

3. Pass the mixture through a sieve into a serving dish and place into the refrigerator. After about a half an hour melt the remaining butter and pour on top, then refrigerate until it's set up (a few more hours).

BUTCHER'S TIP

Cleaning livers isn't complicated but is absolutely necessary. To begin, take the livers out of their packaging and place in a bowl in the sink. Examine all the livers for imperfections like blood spots and fat on the exterior which should all be removed with a paring knife. Give them a thorough rinsing with cold water through a sieve. Now they are ready for sautéing or preparing in your desired manner.

Poaching your pate can be just as simple and the end result just as tasty.

1. After cleaning your chicken livers (as described in the sidebar), place all the ingredients and spices into a bowl or container large enough to handle them all and mix well.

2. Put all your seasoned items into a food processor and blend until a smooth consistency has been achieved.

3. Lay out a small amount of aluminum foil about 12x12 and make logs out of the pate by forming the cylindrical shape with your hands. Roll the foil around the mixture and twist the ends to ensure a tight seal has been formed. Remember, if you make your logs too large you'll have trouble sealing the foil.

4. Tie the ends of the foil-wrapped logs to ensure no water gets in and none of your ingredients seep out.

5. Bring a pot of water large enough to handle multiple pate logs to a simmer (see Figure 9.12). Poach the pate logs for approximately 10 to 15 minutes.

6. Remove the rounds with tongs and allow them to cool to room temperature before putting them into the refrigerator to set up.

7. After they've cooled for a couple of hours you can remove them from the wrap and slice the rounds into ½" slices.

There are so many ways to make use of the offal pieces that would otherwise be wasted. These chapters are just a taste of the many ways to use your home butchery skills in gourmet dishes. Our hope is that as you develop your skills as a home butcher you will move beyond the basic techniques and develop your own unique flair.

Glossary

abattoirs   Slaughterhouses.

aspic   A savory jelly made from meat stock mixed with other ingredients and allowed to set in a mold until gelatinous.

bacon   A cured and smoked pork belly.

baker's scraper   *See* block scraper.

band saw   A large and potentially dangerous piece of equipment that aids in cutting through bone in order to break down a carcass into more manageable cuts and retail cuts of meat.

block scraper   A handheld tool with a flat, thin metal blade, generally not that sharp, that when pushed along a table top will remove any fat buildup or blood remnants.

bologna   *See* Mortadella.

bone saw   A hand saw similar to one you would use to cut wood, but with a food-safe blade and handle.

braising   A cooking method utilizing a lower temperature (275–325°F) in a liquid (stock, wine, water) to prevent the meat from drying out.

breaking   Taking apart a carcass, or "breaking" it down into more manageable cuts.

breaking hook   A metal hook with either a metal, plastic, or sometimes wooden handle that aids in pulling meat to allow a better line of sight while butchering. Generally used while breaking carcasses or primal cuts.

breasola   Salted and air-dried beef eye of round roast.

brining   Submerging meat into a salt/sugar/water solution. The meat then takes on the flavor of the water and remains moist during cooking.

butchering twine   A cotton string that is used to tie roasts into neat, usable cuts.

butchers knot   A string knot that locks in place so the butcher can apply tension on the string in order to form evenly shaped roasts for consistent cooking.

capacola   Dry cured pork shoulder, usually the pork butt.

casing   A vehicle for sausage. Whether natural (beef, pork, or lamb) or synthetic, these are what you use to create links. Sausage is inserted and then twisted into a desired length.

charcuterie   Methods for meat preparation involving salting and air curing or smoking. Originally developed as a form of preservation, now used as a branch or extension of professional kitchens as menu items.

cimeter   Otherwise known as a steak knife. This is a longer bladed knife (usually 10–12″) used to cut larger pieces when a boning knife just won't do the job.

cleaver   A large knife used for cutting through bone. Its heavy blade allows for more force when cutting through chops; aided with a rubber mallet, this tool sometimes eliminates a need for a saw.

curing   Method of food preparation and preservation involving salt, spices, and sometimes nitrates/nitrites.

fermentation   The art form of salting coarsely ground or chopped meat, casing it in natural casings, and hanging it in an area ripe for beneficial bacterial growth. Nitrites are used in this process to aid in the elimination of the growth of botulism.

final cuts   Meat portions that are ready to be cooked.

foie gras   A highly controversial cut of offal. Fattened duck or goose liver. A delicacy in the Western world.

french (as in french the ribs)   Cleaning off the ribs of either a pork rack, beef prime rib, or rack of lamb. This serves two purposes, creating a presentation and removing meat on the bones that will cook faster and eventually burn before the eye of the roast has cooked to a desired internal temperature, therefore creating a burnt or bitter taste.

grass-finished meat   Meat that has been raised on pasture or fed a strict diet of solely grass or hay.

grinder   A butcher shop staple. This piece of equipment ranges in size but performs the same task; meat is guided through a chamber with an auger, and then forced through a metal knife that sits flush to a metal plate. This forms strands of meat, or ground meat.

gristle   The tough bits of connective tissue or "silver skin" that create an unchewable portion of a cut of meat.

gross weight   Weight of the carcass before evisceration.

ham   The hind legs of a pig.

hanging weight   Weight of carcass after evisceration.

"hard on the bone"   When butchering, this refers to keeping your knife as close to the bone as possible.

head cheese   A terrine made from the flesh of a pig's head. Aspic is added and allowed to set up in a terrine mold.

honing   Fine-tuning the edge of your knife.

jerky   Thinly sliced animal meat (bison, beef, elk, etc.) that is seasoned and dried or dehydrated until most of the moisture has been removed.

link   A single determined length of sausage.

maderia   A fortified wine made on the islands of Maderia, Portugal.

membrane   A thin film structure that serves to either allow certain organisms in and keep others out, or simply serve as a barrier of separation.

mortadella   An emulsified sausage heavily seasoned and smoked. Usually found in grocery store deli counters.

offal   Organ meats and overlooked products generally gathered during the evisceration process, such as the liver, heart, kidneys, and intestines.

pancetta   Pork belly that's been salt cured and air dried in a cool climate.

pâté   A mixture of ground or coarsely chopped meats and spices blended together to form either a spreadable paste or a more textured product.

pit master   Someone who operates a barbecue pit.

poach   A method of cooking whereas a food is simmered in warm water to a desired internal temperature that's food safe.

primal cuts   Larger pieces of meat that are initially separated from the carcass. These will go on to become final cuts.

prosciutto   A cured pig's hind leg usually sliced thin and enjoyed as is.

rail breaking   Breaking a carcass from a suspended state. Usually a metal rail track or stationary hook from the ceiling.

rillette   Seasoned meat that is cooked until it's tender enough to shred and then further cooked in fat until it's able to be formed into a paste. Usually served as a spread, similar to pâté.

roast   A cut of meat that's suitable for longer periods of cooking.

sausage   Commonly known as ground meats that have been seasoned and put inside a casing (natural or synthetic) for consumption. Sometimes smoked or cured, these have become a staple of many cultures around the world.

sautéing   A method of cooking whereas an item is pan fried on low heat in either an oil or butter.

scraper (bone scraper)   A handheld tool that removes any "bone dust" or bone material left behind on the meat from using either a bone saw or band saw.

seam   A thin membrane between the muscles that once either loosed by hand or released with a knife, allows you to separate whole muscles intact.

sharpening stone   A stone with different coarsenesses that butchers use to sharpen their knives.

silver skin   A white, almost sliver in appearance, connective tissue that is ever present on beef, pork, and lamb. Whenever possible it should be removed, as it is chewy and inedible.

simmer   A method of cooking in which the food is kept in liquid just below the boiling point until a desired internal temperature is reached.

smoking   A method of cooking in which the meat absorbs the smoke, which then in turn prolongs the life of the meat. First developed in prehistoric times as a matter of preservation, now it is a common, popular cooking method.

steel   Used to hone your knife's edge.

terrines   A food preparation similar to pâtés and rillettes, where the meat is heavily seasoned and cooked for long periods of time. The meat is left in larger chunks or pieces.

trotters   Feet of a pig.

trussing   Tying a piece of meat into a consistent shape for even cooking.

trussing needle   A large needle that resembles a sewing needle. Used to join two or more pieces of meat, making them one larger piece.

vacuum pack machine   Ranging in size, these machines are used to remove oxygen from items; the meat is inserted into a plastic pouch, which is then placed into the vacuum pack chamber where the oxygen is removed. This method prolongs a meat's usability by eliminating oxygen, therefore inhibiting bacterial growth.

white bone   A term for the weakest part of a bone, where you can cut through it with a knife. Found most often at the ends of bones; however, not all bones contain white bone.

Resources for More Information B

This appendix lists some useful websites as well as additional reading material on butchery.

Websites

Butcher & Packer
butcher-packer.com
All your butchery needs—seriously—they have everything but the animals.

Food Safety News
foodsafetynews.com
Keep up-to-date regarding food recalls and other food-related news.

Heritage Foods USA
heritagefoodsusa.com
Specializes in mail-order meats. While they may not sell whole animals, they do sell larger primal cuts.

Local Harvest
localharvest.org
Great resource for farmers markets all over the United States.

Modern Butcher Supply
modernbutchersupply.com
All of your processing equipment needs.

Penzeys Spices
penzeys.com
All your spice needs.

Books

✤ Applestone, Joshua, Applestone, Jessica, and Zissu, Alexandra. *The Butcher's Guide to Well Raised Meat: How to Buy, Cut, and Cook Great Beef, Lamb, Pork, Poultry, and More.* United States: Clarkson Potter, 2011.
The Applestones' no-nonsense approach to running their successful New York butcher shops, Fleisher's. Frank information and great recipes make for a fun and informative read.

✤ Fearnley-Whittingstall, Hugh. *The River Cottage Meat Book.* Berkeley: Berkeley-Ten Speed Press, May 26, 2004.
An amazing look into animal husbandry, sourcing good food animals, and brilliant recipes, to boot. A manifesto for meat eaters everywhere.

✤ McGee, Harold. *On Food and Cooking: The Science and Lore of the Kitchen.* New York City: Scribner, 2004.
An extremely in-depth look at the how and why of cooking. Topics on all food matters are covered. Probably one of the most important food books of all time.

✤ Mettler, John J. *Basic Butchering of Livestock & Game.* United States: Storey Publishing, 1986.
A look at slaughter methods and carcass breakdowns for the homesteader and hunter alike.

✤ Polcyn, Brian, and Michael Ruhlman. *Charcuterie.* New York City: W.W. Norton & Company, 2005.
An authoritative look at the craft of curing from two highly skilled individuals.

✤ Polcyn, Brian, and Michael Ruhlman. *Salumi: The Craft of Italian Dry Curing.* New York City: W.W Norton & Company, 2012.
An in-depth look at Italian curing and its processes.

✤ Wilson, Tim, and Fran Warde. *Ginger Pig Meat Book.* Guilford, CT: Lyons Press, 2011.
Month-to-month accounts of life on a working farm. Great recipes and relevant information for those passionate about their meat.

Tying a Butcher's Knot  C

As with most things in life, a butcher's knot takes on many variations and can be done a number of different ways. In this appendix we are going to break down the lock knot, as it's used the most throughout this book. This knot allows you to get whatever you're tying as tight as your string will possibly allow before it breaks. It's great for trussing up a prime rib or cinching up a cured pork belly for pancetta.

We are going to demonstrate a lock knot on a pork sirloin roast. It should be noted that the photographs are of a right-handed butcher.

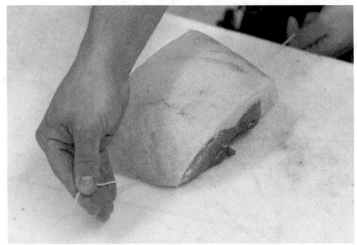

1. With your right hand, take about 4 inches of slack on the string and go under the roast, ensuring a straight and neat line.

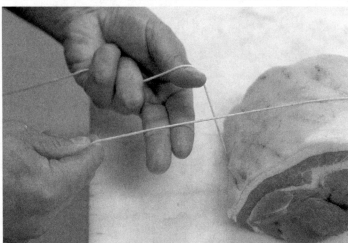

2. Pull the string back over the roast with your right hand and rest the string on your index and middle fingers of your left hand. Note how the string attached to the roll is draped over your left-hand thumb.

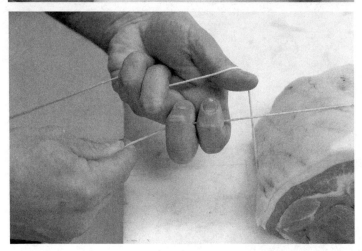

3. Grasp the string tightly with your left index and middle fingers.

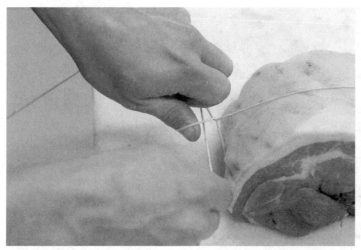

4. Pull the string under and up so the knuckles of your left hand are facing you, still grasping the string. Grasp the string so it's now going around your left fingers.

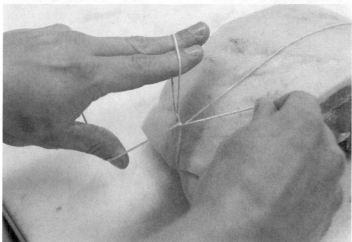

5. Now make a loop by lifting your left fingers upright.

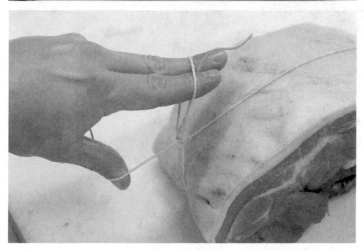

6. With your right hand, take the end of the string and put it between your left index and middle fingers. Hold the end of the string firmly.

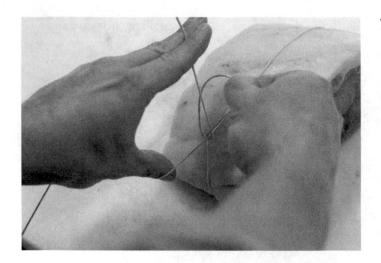

7. Now pull the end of the string through the loop you've created with your left hand.

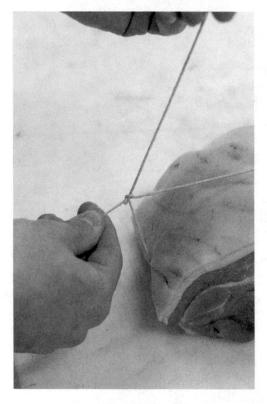

8. With the initial end through the loop, now cinch it tight by pulling the end attached to the roll with your right hand and the slack end with your left. Tighten up the knot by pulling both ends of the string.

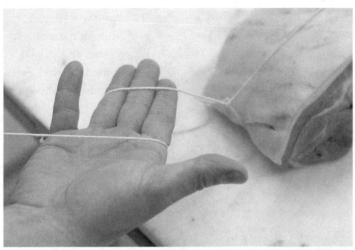

9. Get extra leverage on the roll end of the string by wrapping it around your right hand.

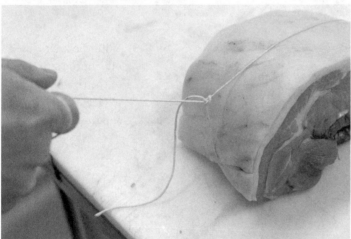

10. With your right hand, pull the string until you feel the "snap." This is the lock taking to the knot and ensures a nice square tie. At this point you can now cinch the knot as tight (or slack) as you like.

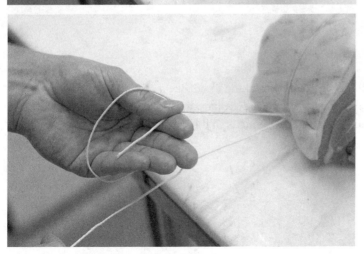

11. Once the knot is to your liking, create a loop with your left hand using the roll end of the string; then take the slack end between your left index finger and thumb.

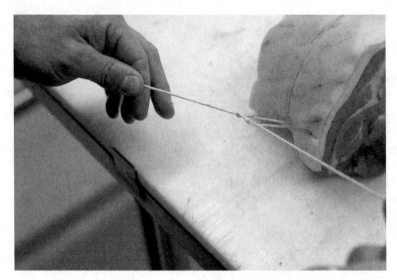

12. Pull the slack end through the loop and tighten up the loop around the slack end to finish off the knot.

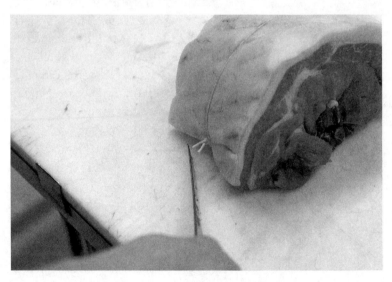

13. With the knot closed off, cut the string close to the finished knot to create a clean visual appearance.

It may seem a bit tricky at first, but soon you'll be making knots like a pro. With a little bit of practice, you'll find it becoming something you don't even have to think about anymore. The more opportunities you have to try your hand at it, the sooner you'll be able to show off your new skill.

Index

E

F

G

L

T